RODALE ORGANIC GARDENING BASICS

pests

RODALE

**From the Editors of
Rodale Organic Gardening
Magazine and Books**

We're always happy to hear from you. For questions or comments concerning the editorial content of this book, please write to:

Rodale Book Readers' Service
33 East Minor Street
Emmaus, PA 18098

Look for other Rodale books wherever books are sold. Or call us at (800) 848-4735.

For more information about Rodale Organic Gardening magazine and books, visit us at:

www.organicgardening.com

Editor: Christine Bucks
Interior Book Designer: Nancy Smola Biltcliff
Interior Illustrator: Tony Davis
Cover Designer: Patricia Field
Cover Photographer: Rob Cardillo
Photography Editor: Lyn Horst
Photography Assistant: Jackie L. Ney
Layout Designer: Dale Mack
Researchers: Diana Erney, Sarah Wolfgang Heffner
Copy Editors: Nancy N. Bailey, Sarah Sacks Dunn
Manufacturing Coordinator: Patrick T. Smith
Indexer: Nan N. Badgett
Editorial Assistance: Kerrie A. Cadden, Claudia Curran

RODALE ORGANIC GARDENING BOOKS
Executive Editor: Kathleen DeVanna Fish
Managing Editor: Fern Marshall Bradley
Executive Creative Director: Christin Gangi
Art Director: Patricia Field
Production Manager: Robert V. Anderson Jr.
Studio Manager: Leslie M. Keefe
Copy Manager: Nancy N. Bailey
Manufacturing Manager: Eileen Bauder

Library of Congress
 Cataloging-in-Publication Data
  Rodale organic gardening basics. Volume 7, Pests / from the editors of Rodale organic gardening magazine and books.
     p.   cm.
    Includes bibliographical references (p.) and index.
    ISBN 0-87596-853-8   (pbk. : alk. paper)
    1. Pests—Biological control.   2. Organic gardening.   I. Title: Pests.   II. Rodale Books. III. Organic gardening (Emmaus, Pa. : 1988) IV. Rodale organic gardening basics ; v. 7.
  SB975 .R62   2001
  632'.96—dc21   00-009602

Distributed in the book trade by St. Martin's Press

2 4 6 8 10 9 7 5 3   paperback

contents

Beating the Bad Guys

When you see a bunch of bugs in your garden, your first instinct is probably to get out a can of pesticide and give 'em a good spraying. After all, everyone's garden is prone to pest problems—and it's either the pests or your plants, right?

Wrong.

The very fact that you have pest insects in your garden means something is out of balance. To figure out what the problem is, you need to look to your plants.

Plants are like people in that if they're too stressed, aren't getting proper nutrition, or living in a place that makes them miserable, they'll get sick. And sick plants are an invitation for bad bugs to move in.

So when you grab that can of toxic pesticide, you aren't solving the problem that brought the bad guys to your garden in the first place. What you are doing, though, is exposing yourself, your family, your pets, and even your plants to harmful chemicals. You're also wiping out the good bugs that hang out in your garden (yes, not all bugs are bad). The good guys are important because they eat the bad bugs and they help pollinate plants.

In the following pages you'll learn about how to prevent plant problems, as well as about all the nonchemical ways of controlling the bugs you don't want—and how to attract the bugs you do want.

Happy organic gardening!

Maria Rodale

Maria Rodale

> **Plants are like people in that if they're too stressed, aren't getting proper nutrition, or living in a place that makes them miserable, they'll get sick.**

By using organic pest-control techniques, you can create a garden that's as beautiful as this one—without risking harm to the plants, the environment, or you.

chapter one

Go Organic: Fighting Pests without Chemicals

Your garden is a natural home for insects—a home where the door is always open. And although you may worry when you spot bugs on your prized vegetables or flowers, the fact is that many insects aren't bad guys at all! They may be in your garden to pollinate flowers or even to prey on plant pests. Of course, you'll want to make sure that the real insect pests that are lurking in the shadows don't take over your garden, but you don't need to use chemicals to keep them in check.

THE BENEFITS OF ORGANIC

Most garden plants are a lot tougher than we might think. They can tolerate some insect damage and still produce lovely flowers or a good crop, which is one reason why spraying pesticides isn't necessary. And if you don't spray pesticides, you won't have to worry about chemicals on the food you're eating. You also don't have to worry about chemicals killing good bugs (also known as beneficials), leaching into the soil, or ending up on the hands (and then subsequently in the mouths) of the neighborhood kids who pick your flowers.

Of course, not using pesticides doesn't mean you just sit back and let the bad guys go to town in your gardens. But if you use organic techniques, you'll be battling destructive insects without harming beneficials, the environment, or you and your family. And don't worry—controlling pests the organic way isn't difficult and won't take up a lot of your time. (Plus, you'll save money not having to buy pesticides!)

> **If you don't spray pesticides, you won't have to worry about chemicals on the food you're eating.**

Adding compost to your beds will give you healthier soil, which in turn will give you healthier plants that will be better able to stand up to bad bugs. And that means you can forgo the pesticides.

Avoid bug zappers because they fry the good bugs as well as the bad ones.

11 THINGS TO STOP DOING NOW!

1. STOP Using Pesticides!

You really *can* grow tasty vegetables and beautiful flowers without using pesticides. Although pesticides kill pests, they also kill helpful organisms that keep your soil rich and healthy. So when you stop using pesticides, you'll have healthier soil, which, in turn, will give you healthier plants. And the healthier your plants are, the better they'll be able to stand up to some insect damage. When you stop using pesticides, there will also be more beneficials around to help eat the bad guys and to pollinate plants. (See "Encouraging the Good Guys" on the opposite page for ways to encourage beneficials to visit your garden.)

2. STOP Using Bug Zappers!

Bug zappers generally do more harm than good because they don't discriminate—they fry beneficial insects as well as destructive insects. Plus, the light from the zappers attracts insects from a considerable distance, so they may increase the numbers of insects (i.e., bad guys) in the vicinity of the light.

3. STOP Giving Pests a Place to Hide!

Many pests seek protection in—and even spend the winter within—garden debris. If you pull out vegetable plants as soon as you finish harvesting, and flowers once they're done blooming, you'll be surprised at the reduction in pest problems you can achieve. And always make sure to pull out any badly infested plants as soon as possible during the growing season.

Make sure to pull out plants—like these sunflowers—as soon as they're done blooming so that pest insects are left out in the cold in winter.

ENCOURAGING THE GOOD GUYS

ENTICING BENEFICIAL INSECTS and animals to your garden is an effective way to control pests—and it's fun, too! You'll enjoy watching a variety of songbirds (they eat lots of insects) on patrol in your garden. And if you're not squeamish about bugs, you'll like observing the wide variety of curious-looking beneficial insects, such as spined soldier beetles and green lacewings, that will frequent your garden. You can encourage predators and parasites that prey on insect pests by doing any or all of the following:

- Put up birdhouses to attract insect-eating birds.
- Plant pollen- and nectar-producing flowers as food sources for beneficial insects.
- Make a shallow water bath for beneficial insects to drink from. Change water every few days, if necessary.
- Leave some mulched areas in your garden undisturbed through the season to provide shelter for beneficials.

Growing a mixture of different plants in your garden will help ward off a pest population explosion.

4. STOP **Planting without Planning!**

Most bugs seek out specific plants, and when they find a large planting of a favorite, they can multiply quickly. If you plant a mix of plants in the garden, it will be harder for the pests to find the crop they want to feast on, so you're less likely to have a bad guy population explosion. You can also include some plants that repel particular pests with odors that the pests dislike. For more information on repellent plants and how they can work for you, see "Preventing Problems" on page 9.

5. STOP **Crowding Plants!**

Crowding plants together can create humid conditions, which can cause some plant diseases. And plants that are sick are a welcome mat for pest insects. You can help promote good air circulation by giving plants adequate space—and by pulling out weeds that creep into your beds.

This colorful caterpillar will eventually turn into a monarch butterfly—a garden good guy.

6. STOP **Killing Every Caterpillar You Find!**

Yes, some caterpillars are pests and can damage your plants. But others are good guys and may actually help your garden by eating their nasty neighbors. So the next time you see a caterpillar, take some time to find out what it is before squashing it.

7. STOP **Growing Pest-Prone Plants!**

As you choose plants for your garden, keep in mind that some plants are less prone to problems than others. For example, many perennial flowers, such as purple coneflower (*Echinacea purpurea*), aren't bothered by pests at all.

Purple coneflower is one perennial that isn't bothered by pests. In fact, beneficial butterflies love its blooms—and seed-eating birds visit its seedheads for snacks in winter.

Adding the right stuff, like vegetable scraps, and keeping out the wrong stuff, like dairy products, will help you produce your own black gold.

8. STOP **Adding the Wrong Stuff to Your Compost Pile!**

A compost pile is an essential part of your organic garden, but don't put meat scraps, dairy products, and other fatty materials such as grease into your pile. These things don't break down easily, and they all attract wildlife, such as pesky raccoons. Dairy products and other fatty ingredients may also trigger the unpleasant development of maggots in your compost.

9. STOP **Overfertilizing!**

Fertilizing with a heavy hand may actually leave some plants susceptible to damage from pests that suck on plants, such as aphids. So before you fertilize, make sure to check the amount that is recommended on the package—and then stick within those guidelines.

10. STOP **Using the Same Fence for All Animal Pests**

All four-legged creatures aren't created equal, meaning one type of fence won't be a cure-all for rabbits, deer, groundhogs, and raccoons. (For example, conventional fencing used to prevent deer from invading your garden should be 8 feet high.) To find out more about fencing to keep out these specific animals (and for how to figure out which ones are invading your garden in the first place), see "Animal Pests" on page 79.

11. STOP Planting the Same Vegetables in the Same Place Every Year!

Changing what you plant in a particular garden spot from year to year (called crop rotation) can help fight pests, too. Some pests, like the corn rootworm, lay their eggs at the base of a particular vegetable plant—in this case, corn. But rootworm larvae feed only on corn and can't travel far to find food. So when the eggs hatch the following year, if there's no corn growing in the same spot, the new generation of insects won't be able to find anything to eat.

Avoid planting corn in the same place every year to help foil the corn rootworm.

The key to preventing pest problems is to start with healthy plants.

chapter two

Preventing Problems

What's better than defeating a horde of plant-munching pests? Stopping those pests before they take their first bite. You can foil pests' dining plans by making sure your plants are as healthy as possible. And that includes carefully choosing your planting site, providing good general gardening care, and cleaning up your garden in the fall. You can also help keep your plants healthy by encouraging beneficial insects—the natural enemies of pests—to hang out in your garden.

CHOOSING THE RIGHT SITE

Although you may not realize it, where you grow your plants can have an impact on how well (or not so well) they stand up to pest problems. That's why choosing the right site is so important. If you put your plants where they'll do their best, they'll be healthier and less susceptible to pests—and better able to fight off any bad guys that do show up.

Start by learning what you can about your local climate, then study your yard to learn the special conditions it offers. Depending on whether you're growing vegetables or flowers (or both), you'll need to keep certain points in mind when choosing the right site.

> **If you put your plants where they'll do their best, they'll be healthier and less susceptible to pests.**

A Site for Vegetables

- Choose a site with daylong full sun. Most vegetables (and herbs) need a minimum of 6 hours of direct sun every day. They'll grow with less sun, but yields will be lower and the plants will be less vigorous—an invitation to pests to attack!

- Look for a spot with good air circulation. Avoid sites closed in on all sides by buildings or dense vegetation. Poor air circulation is an open door to disease, and sick plants are a welcome mat for pests.

BUILDING RAISED BEDS

RAISED BEDS are a great solution for planting vegetables in soggy sites. They offer good drainage as well as better aeration than ground-level beds.

The quickest way to make a raised bed is by mounding. After removing weeds or sod from your chosen site, work the soil with a fork to loosen it, heap compost and well-rotted manure on top, and then rake it together to create a mounded bed. (Try to keep the width of the bed between 4 and 5 feet, so that you can comfortably reach to the middle without having to walk on it.) You can also frame raised beds to keep the soil from eroding (this will have the added bonus of creating nicer-looking beds). Wood, rocks, bricks, or cinder blocks are all good materials for framing raised beds. Avoid using pressure-treated wood because it contains toxic materials that may leach into the soil.

- Make sure the site has adequate drainage because many vegetables can't tolerate wet soil. Too much water will cause plants to rot, making them more susceptible to bad bugs. If you must deal with a wet site, build raised growing beds to improve drainage. (See "Building Raised Beds" on this page.)

- Keep your garden as far as possible from trees, which have widely spreading root systems that consume huge amounts of water. If your plants have to compete with trees for water, they probably won't get as much as they need. Lack of water will lead to stress, which, in turn, will make them more vulnerable to pests.

A Site for Flowers

- For flowers, you can choose either a sunny site or a shady site; there are plenty of flowers that like sun and many others that do well in shade. Just be sure you plant flowers in the proper light conditions so that they will grow their best. (Remember, the healthier your plants, the better equipped they'll be to withstand pests.) For example, you might grow astilbes and hostas in a shady corner, and plant sunflowers and zinnias in a bright, sunny spot.

- After you pick your site, check the soil pH, and assess whether the site is windy or sheltered, wet or dry. Then choose plants based on your soil and site conditions. Although you can probably make some small-scale changes, it's wise to choose mainly plants that will thrive in the soil and climate that you already have.

- If you need to modify your site, such as to create a more acid soil or install a windbreak, group plants that need this change together in one area so they will all benefit.

Always plant flowers in a site where they'll do their best. Here, dianthus, petunias, and salvia enjoy basking in the bright sun.

COMPACTED SOIL

COMPACTED OR HEAVILY cultivated soil may have an impermeable layer, called a hardpan, lurking beneath its surface. Hardpan reduces water drainage and limits plants' ability to establish deep roots. If a hardpan layer is close to the soil surface, you may be able to break it up by working the soil deeply.

If your soil is simply compacted, loosen it as deeply as possible and add compost and other bulky organic materials. Soon earthworms will improve the soil.

Rocky soil makes it harder to dig planting holes, but it should be fine for permanent plantings of trees, shrubs, and perennials. On sites such as vegetable gardens and annual flowerbeds where you plan to cultivate more often, you may need to remove the rocks to make the soil workable.

WELCOMING GOOD BUGS

Growing plants that attract beneficials—natural enemies of pest insects—is another way to help you fight the bad guys without chemicals. Among the beneficial insects flying about your garden are lacewings, lady beetles (otherwise known as ladybugs), parasitic miniwasps, syrphid flies, and tachinid flies. To encourage beneficials, try the following strategies:

Provide nectar and pollen. Many beneficial insects eat nectar and pollen as well as insects. But because beneficials have short mouthparts, they can't reach deeply into flowers for food. Plants with numerous small flowers containing easy-to-reach pollen and nectar provide the high-protein and high-sugar meals that beneficial insects need. Daisies, dill, fennel, mint, and mustard are just a few of the common plants that beneficial insects favor.

Make a bug bath. Water is important to all creatures, including bugs. To provide a water source for beneficials, fill a shallow dish with small stones. Then add enough water to create shallow pools among the stones. Many beneficial insects are tiny and can drown easily, so be sure your insect baths have dry landing sites and

Invite good bugs into your garden by growing plants they love, such as (counterclockwise from top right) yarrow, goldenrod, sweet alyssum, and daisies.

only shallow water. If you garden in an area that's very humid or rainy in the summer, the natural moisture from rain or morning dew may be all the water your beneficials need.

Don't use pesticides. The single step that will most increase your garden's population of helpers is limiting or eliminating the use of pesticides.

Reduce dust. Plant a hedge or build a windbreak fence around your garden to reduce dust; beneficial insects dehydrate easily in dusty conditions.

Offer protection. Permanent pathways and mulched beds are protected areas where beneficials can hide from predators.

HERBS THAT REPEL

PLANTING HERBS as companion plants in the vegetable or flower garden is a time-honored (but not infallible) way of helping to deter some pests. Here's a list of some of the most useful herbs for repelling pests.

Anise: Repels aphids

Artemisia: Repels flea beetles, cabbageworms, slugs

Basil: Repels flies and other insects

Catnip: Repels ants, flea beetles

Coriander: Repels aphids

Garlic: Repels aphids, Japanese beetles

Mint: Repels aphids, flea beetles, cabbage pests

Pot marigold: Repels asparagus beetles

Summer savory: Repels Mexican bean beetles

Tansy: Repels ants, Japanese beetles, flies

Although catnip may invite a cat to your garden, it will keep ants and flea beetles out.

PROVIDING THE BEST CARE

Another key part of keeping plants problem-free is giving them good general care. Poor growing conditions can stress your plants and make them more problem-prone. Both under- and overwatering, for instance, can create problems for your plants. Overwatered plants are more likely to develop root diseases; underwatered plants will be stunted and more susceptible to sucking insects and mites. Most plants need to dry out a bit between waterings, but some tolerate or even need a longer drying-out period than others. If you're not sure about what growing conditions are best for your plants, take a look at a good plant reference book to find out what they like—see "Recommended Reading & Resources" on page 99 for some suggestions. (Experience is also a good teacher—the more you garden, the more you'll find out what works and what doesn't.)

Other ways to provide good garden care include:

Go easy on the food. Overfertilized plants become somewhat more susceptible to being attacked by sucking pests, such as aphids. To avoid overfertilizing, use restraint when applying concentrated fertilizers like guano and wood ashes, especially to soil in containers, and never apply more than the recommended amount. Before you fertilize, be sure your plants are actively growing and that the soil is moist.

Give plants room. Planting flowers or vegetables too close together

You can help take the pest welcome sign off your garden door by keeping your garden weed-free—so pests have fewer places to hide.

can also foster problems because crowded plants must compete with each other for light, water, and nutrients—thus stressing them and making them more susceptible to pest attacks.

Don't let weeds go unchecked. Weeds crowd plants and serve as alternative hosts for insect pests.

Rotate crops. Rotating vegetable crops—changing their position in the garden from year to year—is another cultural practice that can reduce some pest problems. This technique works best, though, if you have a large garden. In a small garden, you may not be able to move a crop far enough from its last planting site to avoid the insect that caused the problem.

Choose resistance. You can stack the deck in your favor before you start the garden season by choosing vegetable varieties that are resistant to pests. Take the time to hunt out varieties that can resist the pests you know are common in your area—it will save you the woe of fighting those pests all season long. (If you're not sure what pests are commonly found in your area, call your local county extension service agent.)

Keep things clean. Cleaning up garden debris— such as spent plants and fallen foliage—weekly helps to eliminate pests' hiding places.

Finding the Bad Guys

Another part of providing good plant care is regularly looking for pests. Follow these four guidelines to find problem bugs early—when they're easiest to control.

Do it on purpose. You might come upon problem pests during a casual stroll through your garden, but you're more likely to miss most of the bad guys. Instead, set aside about 10 minutes during your garden visit to concentrate on looking for signs of pests, like irregular holes in your cabbage leaves (imported cabbageworms) or large holes in the leaves and flowers of roses (Japanese beetles).

3 KEYS TO HEALTHY PLANTS

A LITTLE PEST DAMAGE is just a natural part of organic gardening—but if you're having major problems, take a moment to step back and examine how you're feeding and watering your vegetables. That's because the stronger and healthier your plants are, the fewer problems you'll have with pests. To assure strong and healthy plants:

- Fertilize with compost on a regular basis.

- Get a soil test every few years to determine whether you need to add any extra amendments to your soil.

- Be sure to provide plenty of water. Plant roots can absorb nutrients only when there is ample moisture in the soil.

WINTER SURVIVAL

KNOWING HOW AND WHERE pest insects spend the winter can give you important clues about how to control them. Many adult insects can't survive the winter, but often their eggs, larvae, or pupae can withstand a long cold period in a state of hibernation. Many pests, during their overwintering stage, burrow deep into the soil or into litter (fallen leaves, mulch, and so on) on the ground, where they're protected form inclimate temperatures.

Cultivating the soil in early spring can expose these hidden hibernators to predators like birds. Other pests, such as leafrollers and tent caterpillars, pupate or lay eggs in cracks and crevices in tree bark. Scraping egg masses off bark and spraying trees with dormant oil in early spring can help to eliminate the pests before they begin damaging the new season's growth.

Stick to a schedule. Scout for bad guys twice a week, at different times of the day. If you decide to check plants in the morning this weekend, for instance, make your next inspection in the evening in the middle of the week.

Be a smart sampler. Instead of inspecting every plant, you can save time by thoroughly examining every fourth or fifth plant. If you have a large garden, check several plants on the outside and several on the inside of the bed.

Keep records. Insect activity can vary with the weather and season, but there will often be a consistent pattern from one year to the next. If you note when you begin seeing common pests this year, next year's scouting may be a lot easier.

CLEANING UP

Fall cleanup plays a role in preventing outbreaks of many kinds of insect pests that overwinter in specific plants. Even a few overwintering insects can lead to an outbreak the following year. Cleaning up dying asparagus stalks, for instance, removes overwintering asparagus beetles, while turning under cornstalks will destroy European corn borer larvae, which overwinter in the stem. Some simple cleanup guidelines include:

- Pull or cut weeds before they can form seed.
- Pull out spent vegetable plants after they're finished bearing.
- Collect stakes, temporary trellises, and row covers, and scrape off clinging soil. To remove insect eggs, rinse the materials in a solution of 1 part bleach and 9 parts water. Spread the materials out to dry in the sun before storing them.
- Pick any remaining vegetables.
- Mulching is another way to kill pests that spend the winter in the soil, particularly Colorado potato beetles. Mulch in the fall, pull back the mulch for 3 days during very cold weather, then replace the mulch in spring.

quick tip

After your vegetables are finished producing, pull the plants from the garden. Check their roots for signs of disease and insects. Bury any plants that show signs of disease or infestation, or dispose of them in your household trash. You should toss anything else onto your compost pile.

Fall cleanup—including pulling out spent plants and cutting weeds—is key to preventing pest problems the following season.

Your pest-fighting arsenal should be made up of basic supplies, such as a floating row cover.

chapter three

Pest-Stopping Supplies

Your arsenal against insect pests doesn't have to be large—a few basic supplies such as floating row covers and insecticidal soap are effective, nonchemical ways to help you fight the battle. You can also use low-tech methods, such as spraying water or hand-picking, to get pests to put up the white flag and surrender.

GATHERING WHAT YOU'LL NEED

Despite what your neighbor says (or does), you don't need to wage a chemical war against bad bugs. It's true—you really *can* get the upper hand on pests without ever introducing chemicals into your garden. As we mentioned earlier, fighting pests without chemicals isn't difficult. And it isn't overly time-consuming, either.

To make the most of your pest-fighting time, though, you'll need some key supplies, which are listed on this page. You should be able to purchase most of these products at a garden center, but if not, you can order them by mail (see "Recommended Reading & Resources" on page 99 for more information). In addition to these materials, you'll find two pieces of equipment helpful in your quest to conquer the bad guys: a hand lens and a sprayer.

A hand lens is useful for identifying insects, especially those that are difficult to see with the naked eye. It's important to know what bugs are in your garden so you'll know what methods will best get rid of them—*and* so that you don't end up killing beneficials just because you thought they were bad guys.

You'll need a sprayer (which you can get at a garden supply center) for applying insecticidal soap, horticultural oils, and some forms of BT.

6 Essential Pest-Fighting Supplies

- **Floating row covers**
- ***Bacillus thuringiensis* (BT)**
- **Sticky traps and bands**
- **Pheromone traps**
- **Insecticidal soap**
- **Horticultural oils**

FLOATING ROW COVERS

One of the best ways to protect your plants from pests is to use a barrier, such as a floating row cover. Placed over plants, this translucent, white, fabriclike material keeps insects out but allows water and light to pass through. You can cut the material into small squares for individual plants, or leave it in large pieces to cover a garden bed. You can also use floating row covers two different ways to keep out pests.

The first way you can use them is as temporary protection for plants when they're at a critical stage of growth. This is often the seedling or young transplant stage, but it could be a later period when a pest is active. For this purpose, drape the row cover loosely over the plants, and bury the edges of the material on all sides under the soil. Remove the cover when the plants are large enough to withstand damage or when pests are no longer a problem.

The second way to use them is as a barrier during a crop's entire growing season. To cover just a few plants or a few square feet, you can make a removable rectangular frame of wood or PVC tubing. Be sure the frame is tall enough to accommodate the mature plants. Cover the sides and top of the frame with the row cover, securing the edges with staples or tape. Put the frame over the seedbed or transplants, pushing it firmly into the soil surface. Lift the frame as needed to check on the progress of the crop or to harvest.

quick tip

If you cover a crop that's pollinated by insects, such as squash or cucumbers, make sure to uncover the plants when they start to flower. If you don't, the pollinators won't be able to do their job, and you'll end up with nothing to harvest.

BT

Bacillus thuringiensis (often referred to as BT) is a bacterium that causes some types of pests to get sick and die after they ingest it. When susceptible pests eat a BT-sprayed leaf or BT-treated bait, they stop eating and soon die. BT comes in different strains: *B. thuringiensis* var. *kurstaki* (BTK) kills a number of caterpillar pests, including cabbageworms and tomato hornworms; *B. thuringiensis* var. *san diego* controls pest beetles, including black vine weevils and Colorado potato beetles. BT comes in the following forms:

- Liquids you dilute and put into a sprayer
- Dusts or granules that you apply directly to plants
- Powders that you mix with water before applying with a sprayer

Timing Is Everything

Applying BT is most effective when pests are very young—in the larval stage. If you first notice the pests when most of them are adults or large larvae, you should try another control method. Also, BT loses its effectiveness just 1 to 4 days after it's applied, so you must time your applications well. Some other points to keep in mind when using BT are as follows:

- Spray BT in the morning or evening, but not during the heat of the day. Most insects don't feed at midday, and BT breaks down quickly when exposed to sunlight.

- Use BT sparingly—and only on plants you know have susceptible pests—because in some cases, pest caterpillars have become resistant to it.

- Keep BT cool to prolong its storage life; BT powders, liquids, and dusts kept at 70°F will stay fresh for 2 to 3 years.

- If the BT you're using needs to be mixed with water, mix only as much as you plan to use that same day— BT starts to break down as soon as it's mixed.

quick tip

If you decide to use BT to battle pests, handle all products with care. BT can cause allergic reactions in some people when inhaled or rubbed into the skin. Anyway, it's not a good idea to breathe any kind of dust or mist that you're using in the garden. So wear long sleeves and pants, and don goggles and a mask when spraying BT.

Products that contain Bacillus thuringiensis (BT) are effective in wiping out the larval stage of many bad bugs.

STICKY TRAPS AND STUFF

Sticky traps catch insects that are attracted to a specific color, or, in the case of red sphere traps, to a specific color and shape.

Yellow sticky traps attract aphids, gnats, leafminers, scale, and whiteflies, just to name a few.

Bright blue traps attract thrips.

White traps attract tarnished plant bugs (they also attract beneficial flies, so you should use them only early in the season).

Yellowish orange traps attract carrot rust flies.

Red spheres covered with sticky glue attract female apple maggots.

You can buy commercial sticky traps or make your own out of wood, cardboard, or stiff plastic. All you need to do is cover the base with a coat of primer and two coats of paint. (Of course, the color you choose

Red ball sticky traps hung in apple trees are deceivingly deadly to some apple pests.

depends on what sorts of pests you're trying to catch.) Then, using a paintbrush or knife, coat the base with a sticky compound, such as Tanglefoot (a nontoxic vegetable-based product), and hang it in your garden. When the trap is full of insects, scrape them off and recoat the trap.

Sticky band traps are another type of pest trap. These traps work for crawling pests like gypsy moth caterpillars. To apply a sticky band to a tree, wrap plastic kitchen wrap around the trunk and spread a band of sticky coating on the plastic. When the plastic gets full of insects, take it off the tree, dispose of it, and put on a fresh band.

PHEROMONES

Pheromones are chemical cues that insects use to communicate with others of their species. Female insects produce sex pheromones that waft into the air and attract males, who follow the direction of the pheromone until they find a mate. Synthetic pheromones are available in long-lasting lures and are widely used in sticky traps to monitor pest populations. When enough pheromone traps are used, they can control the population by trapping so many males that a significant portion of the females go unmated and don't lay eggs.

The traps are usually a wing or triangular shape and are open and coated with a sticky substance inside. Once the pests enter the trap (in search of a female) and touch the inner surface, they're stuck.

Pheromone lures such as this one invite male pests in—and then stick it to 'em once they're inside.

HOMEMADE TRAPS

YOU CAN MAKE a simple trap to use with a pheromone lure using an item you probably have at home: a 1-quart plastic ice cream or yogurt container. Cut three large holes in the upper half of the container's sides. If the lid isn't opaque, paint it or line it with cardboard to shade the lure. Tape a commercial lure to the inside of the lid.

Then, push a sturdy stake into the ground in your garden, and fasten the trap to the stake. Fill the bottom half of the container with soapy water and snap on the lid with the lure attached. Insects attracted by the pheromone will fly inside the trap and end up drowning in the soapy water. Check the trap every few days and replace the soapy water after it's filled with pests.

Keep the following points in mind when using pheromone traps:

- Set out the traps about 2 or 3 weeks before you expect the target pest to emerge (one trap is usually enough for a home garden). Check them every couple of days or once a week.

- Make sure to follow the package directions.

- If you're using Japanese beetle traps, don't put the traps too close to their favorite plants (like roses), or else you may end up inviting *more* beetles to feed on the plants.

You can also control insect population explosions by what's called "mating disruption." Putting out lots of pheromone lures (usually on twist-ties impregnated with pheromones) saturates the air with these chemical cues. Once the air is saturated, male insects can't locate females to mate with them.

INSECTICIDAL SOAP

Insecticidal soap is a mild spray that kills insect pests like aphids, mites, and whiteflies. You can buy commercial soap spray or make your own homemade spray. Commercial soap sprays are toxic to pests and harmless to plants. Household soaps are more likely to injure plants. Keep these points in mind when using insecticidal soap:

You can make your own soap spray with household dish soap and water.

- Check the label of commercial soaps carefully before spraying. If the plant you want to treat isn't listed, apply the soap spray to only a few leaves, then wait 48 hours to see if they are damaged before you spray the whole plant.

- Spray plants every 3 to 7 days for mild infestations; spray every 2 or 3 days for bad ones.

- Mix the soap with soft water.

SKIP THESE CONTROLS

ORGANIC GARDENING BOOKS used to recommend potent botanical insecticides, such as nicotine, pyrethrum, rotenone, ryania, and sabadilla. The advantage of using botanicals—insecticides derived from plants—over chemical pesticides is that they break down within a few days after they're applied. This means that beneficial insects (the good guys) are at risk for a relatively short period, long-term contamination of the environment is unlikely, and botanicals probably won't persist as residues on food we grow. So, what're some of the downsides of these botanicals?

- Before it breaks down, nicotine is one of the most toxic poisons known.

- Pyrethrums are toxic to beneficial insects and cold-blooded animals like fish and amphibians. They can also cause allergic reactions and skin rashes in some people.

- Rotenone, ryania, and sabadilla are also very toxic. They can kill bees (and in the case of rotenone, birds and fish) as well as pests.

- Rotenone, ryania, and sabadilla are moderately toxic to pets and people. They also pose a risk to the person applying the product, especially if the person is not wearing protective clothing, gloves, and a mask.

Because many effective, nontoxic methods of managing all kinds of pest problems are available today, we no longer endorse using these botanicals. With the prevention and control techniques recommended in this book, you'll get excellent pest control without having to resort to any of the older botanicals.

Forget about using botanical insecticides. Some are extremely toxic and can kill beneficials, like bees.

● If you make your own soap, use 1 to 3 teaspoons of household dish soap (not detergent) per gallon of water. Keep in mind that the effectiveness of soap will vary from brand to brand.

HORTICULTURAL OILS

Horticultural oils smother insect eggs and some types of immature insects. There are two categories of oils: dormant and summer.

Dormant oil is a heavy petroleum oil that you can spray on dormant plants to control overwintering pests such as aphids, mites, and scale. Spray a 1 to 3 percent mixture of oil in water when the air tempera-ture is above 40°F. Certain plants (such as Japanese maples) are very sensitive and can be severely dam-aged by dormant oil. Before spraying the whole plant, spray a small area and see if yellowing occurs.

Help keep your summer flowerbeds looking this good by controlling aphids and spider mites with summer oil.

Summer oil, also called superior or supreme oil, is a lighter petroleum oil that contains fewer of the impurities that make dormant oil toxic to plants. This oil controls aphids, some caterpillars, mealybugs, scale, and spider mites. Spray a mixture of up to 2 percent summer oil in water when the air temperature is below 85°F and the plants aren't drought- or heat-stressed. Test a small area on a plant first, wait a few days, and if there are no signs of spotting or discoloration, spray thoroughly.

quick tip

As a substitute for summer oil, you can use 1 tablespoon of plain vegetable oil and ¼ teaspoon of liquid soap per quart of water. Shake vigorously and spray.

FREE PEST-CONTROL SUPPLIES

Controlling pests doesn't have to involve costly or high-tech supplies and equipment. In fact, water, empty toilet-paper tubes, and a packet of seeds can all be used for controlling pests. Here's how.

Use water as a pesticide. A strong spray of water from a garden hose can be a surprisingly effective controller of aphids, small caterpillars, mites, and scale. Repeat sprays as needed.

Ring your seedlings. Simple barriers are very effective at protecting young seedlings from pests. Cardboard tubes (empty toilet-paper cylinders or paper-towel tubes) cut into smaller sections or aluminum foil collars will keep pests from chewing tender stems. A 4-inch

Aluminum foil collars will help protect the stems of young plants from pests such as cutworms.

A sacrificial trap crop of early squash (top) can help you nab the bad guys. Fennel (above) attracts tiny wasps that snack on pests.

square of cardboard laid flat on the soil surface surrounding broccoli, cabbage, and cauliflower seedlings will prevent nasty cabbage root maggot adults from laying their eggs.

Plant a trap. Bugs prefer certain predictable foods. So by planting a few sacrificial "trap" veggies, you can lure them away from the vegetables you want, and then either sacrifice the trap crop or nab the bad guys while they feast. Certain flea beetles, for example, love radishes and Chinese cabbage; you can use mustard as a trap crop to lure nasty harlequin bugs. And you can start some plants of summer squash in pots and set them out in the garden a few weeks before you plant your main squash crop, and then destroy the beetles attracted to the plants.

Invite beneficials in. Get good bugs like lady beetles, tachinid flies, and green lacewings to work for you—the more beneficials you have, the fewer pests. You can increase the good guy numbers by planting lots of flowers and allowing herbs to flower in and around your garden. Coriander, dill, and fennel, for example, attract tiny wasps that feast on many pests; white sweet alyssum attracts aphid-eating hoverflies and other beneficials.

A BIT ABOUT BUGS

WHEN IS A BUG not a bug? Scientists would tell you that "bugs" are a class of insect that has sucking mouthparts and a certain type of wing structure. But to most people, bugs include a mixed bag of creepy critters, including insects, mites, nematodes, sowbugs, pillbugs, millipedes, centipedes, slugs, and snails. Most of these creatures are arthropods, which means they have a hard-shelled body and jointed legs. The exceptions are nematodes—a kind of worm—and slugs and snails.

You know about the miraculous transformation of caterpillars into butterflies. Most insects have life cycles with a similar pattern. Adult insects lay eggs, and then the adults usually die. The eggs hatch as soft-bodied larvae. Caterpillars are butterfly larvae, while beetle larvae are generally called grubs, and fly larvae are maggots. The larvae feed awhile and then go into a resting state—a pupa or cocoon. The adults emerge from the cocoon and feed some more. Then they mate, and the cycle starts again. There are hundreds of variations on the cycle, but the basic pattern is the same.

Insect life cycles can be short—just a few weeks—or they can be long, even taking years. For insects with more than one generation a year, the number of generations varies with the length of the growing season. This means that there are usually fewer generations in northern regions than in the South. An insect's growth rate depends on the temperature of its environment, so a generation takes longer to mature in spring and fall than in summer. In unusually warm weather or long growing seasons, you may find some pests will squeeze in an extra generation in your garden.

Unlike these Japanese beetles, most of the bugs in your garden aren't harmful, which is why it's important to identify a bug before wiping it out.

chapter four

Bad Bugs

Distinguishing bad bugs from the good guys can be difficult, especially since bad bugs don't carry tiny flags with the word "pest" written on them. But while lots of insects may reside in your garden, most of them aren't harmful. That's why you should use the following guide to help you identify a suspected pest before you decide to do it in.

LIGHT SNACKING IS OK

Even when you find pests in your garden, keep in mind that most of their snacking doesn't particularly endanger your vegetables, flowers, or landscape plantings. As we mentioned back in Chapter 1, your plants can tolerate some damage. For example, holes in the leaves of a potato plant or an apple tree only affect the crop's yield if quite a bit of damage is done. For this type of pest, you might not need to do any-thing, or you may need to do something only in years with particularly heavy outbreaks. Many insect popula-tions rise and fall over a period of years, so outbreaks over a few years may be followed by several years without damage.

Preventing pest damage is easier than treating your plants.

Planning Ahead

Although you'll find descriptions of more than 20 pests on the following pages, don't be intimidated! They won't all reside in your garden. Only a few are a problem for any given plant or region of the country. Once you find out which pests are regular problems where you live, the best thing you can do is to plan ahead to prevent the problems next year. Preventing pest damage is easier and more effective than treating your plants or trying to control the pests after the damage occurs.

APHIDS

Actual size ¹⁄₁₆" to ³⁄₈" long

Damage
Aphids feed on plant sap, which causes leaves to curl and turn yellow. Buds, branch tips, and flowers may also become distorted.

= range

Aphids are soft, pear-shaped, and very tiny (¹⁄₁₆ to ³⁄₈ inch long). Two short tubes project backward from the tip of their abdomen. Aphids have long antennae. Some types of aphids have wings, which are transparent, longer than their body, and held like a roof over their back. Aphids may be green, pink, yellowish, black, or powdery gray. Nymphs resemble adults but are smaller and wingless.

Where They Live
You'll find aphids throughout North America.

Their Life Cycle
Aphids reproduce like there's no tomorrow. Female aphids can reproduce without mating, giving birth

continuously to live nymphs. Nymphs mature in 1 to 2 weeks and start producing offspring themselves.

When days become shorter in the fall, both males and females are born. They mate, and then females lay eggs on stems or in bark crevices. The eggs overwinter and hatch the following spring. In very mild climates and in greenhouses, aphids may reproduce year-round.

Plants They Attack

Aphids feed on most fruit and vegetable plants, flowers, ornamentals, and shade trees.

Why They're a Problem

Both adults and nymphs suck plant sap, which usually causes distorted leaves, buds, branch tips, and flowers. Severely infested leaves and flowers may drop. As they feed, aphids excrete a sweet, sticky honeydew onto the leaves below. This allows a sooty mold to grow, which, in addition to being ugly to look at, blocks light from leaves. Also, some aphids spread viruses as they feed.

Organic Damage Control

- Drench plants with strong sprays of water from a garden hose to kill aphids. (A hard, driving rainstorm will have the same effect.)

- Keep your plants as healthy as possible, and spray dormant oil to control overwintering eggs on fruit trees.

- Attract predators by planting pollen and nectar plants such as yarrow and sweet alyssum.

- Control ants that guard aphid colonies in trees from predators by placing sticky bands around the trunks.

- Spray aphids with insecticidal soap, summer oil (on tolerant plants), and homemade garlic sprays.

quick tip

A homemade garlic spray is useful for combating aphids. To make, finely chop 10 to 15 garlic cloves and soak the pieces in 1 pint of mineral oil for 24 hours. Strain and spray as is, or dilute with water and add a few drops of soap.

BLACK VINE WEEVILS

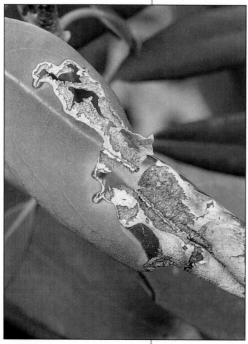

Actual size ⅓" long

Damage
Most plants can withstand the feeding of adult black vine weevils, which leave their characteristic scalloped notches along leaf edges; however, the larvae feed on roots, which can stunt or kill plants.

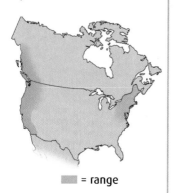

= range

Adult weevils are oval, brownish gray or black, and ⅓ inch long. They have a pattern of small yellow patches on their backs. Their larvae are fat, white grubs that are up to ½ inch long with yellowish brown heads.

Where They Live

You'll find black vine weevils in the northeastern United States, as well as from California to the Pacific Northwest.

Their Life Cycle

For weevils, reproducing is solely women's work, as there are only female weevils—no males. The adults emerge from the soil in June and feed for several weeks before laying eggs in the soil around host plants.

The eggs hatch in about 10 days and the larvae immediately burrow into the roots to feed for the rest of the season. They stay in the soil over the winter, then resume feeding on roots the following spring. The larvae pupate in early spring, completing the cycle.

Plants They Attack

Black vine weevils most commonly attack blackberry, blueberry, cranberry, and strawberry plants, as well as some ornamentals, particularly azaleas, camellias, rhododendrons, wisterias, and yews.

Why They're a Problem

Weevils chew along leaf edges, leaving small, scalloped bite marks. Adults rarely cause serious damage, but larvae can be very damaging because they feed on plant roots. Their feeding stunts plant growth and may indirectly kill plants by allowing disease organisms to enter injured roots.

Organic Damage Control

- At night, when they feed, knock weevils off plants onto a sheet on the ground and destroy them. (If you don't want to squish them, you can just drop them in a bucket of soapy water and drown them.)

- Lay boards under plants and check for weevils hiding under them during the day.

- Plant resistant rhododendron and azalea varieties that have rolled leaf edges, which prevent weevils from grasping an edge to feed.

- Intercept weevils as they climb shrubs by tying a 6-inch-high band of plastic wrap painted with sticky trap glue around the trunk.

- Add bird-friendly shrubs, birdbaths, and feeders to your landscape—birds and other predators find black vine weevils delicious.

quick tip

If you have heavy weevil infestations, try trapping adults starting in April. Set out stakes wrapped with 12-inch-high corrugated plastic or cardboard. Remove paper from one side of the cardboard and face the corrugations inward. Check these every few days and destroy all weevils that accumulate.

CABBAGE LOOPERS

Actual size 1½" long

Damage
When you see holes chewed in your cabbage, broccoli, or other cole crops, look closely and you're likely to find a cabbage looper camouflaged among the leaves.

= range

Cabbage looper adults are mottled gray-brown moths with a silvery, V-shaped spot in the middle of each forewing. Their wingspan is 1½ inches. Because they fly late in the evening, you rarely see them. Their larvae are green caterpillars with pairs of wavy, white or light yellow lines down their backs and one line along each side.

Where They Live

Cabbage loopers are found throughout North America.

Their Life Cycle

Adult moths emerge in May from their overwintering cocoons to lay eggs. The eggs hatch in 3 or 4 days and the larvae feed for 2 to 3 weeks. They pupate for up to 2 weeks in thin silk cocoons attached to the stems or undersides of leaves. Three or four generations of cabbage loopers may appear in a year, depending on where you live.

Plants They Attack

As you might expect, cabbage loopers attack mainly cabbage and cabbage-family plants. They'll also feed on beets, celery, lettuce, peas, spinach, tomatoes, and flowers, including carnations and nasturtiums.

Why They're a Problem

Cabbage looper caterpillars damage plants by chewing large holes in leaves. If you have lots of them, they can ruin whole plants. Larvae are most damaging during the last few days of their development.

Organic Damage Control

● Handpick caterpillars several times a week and spray *Bacillus thuringiensis* var. *kurstaki* (BTK) as well.

● Attract predatory and parasitic insects to the garden with pollen and nectar plants.

● If you live in the North, start your cabbage indoors and put the plants out in the garden very early to avoid peak populations.

● At the end of the season, bury spent cabbage plants to destroy cocoons before adults emerge in spring.

● Many native parasites and predators attack cabbage loopers. Invite these helpers into your garden by planting flowers for them to feed on when loopers are not prevalent. Beneficial insects prefer tiny flowers like those that make up the large, flat umbels of parsley, dill, fennel, and coriander. Alyssum and tansy are also known to attract beneficials.

quick tip

Conduct cabbage looper search-and-destroy missions during the brightest part of the day—it's much easier to spot loopers when plants are dry. When water beads up on the waxy leaves of cabbage and broccoli, spotting these pests is more difficult.

CABBAGE MAGGOTS

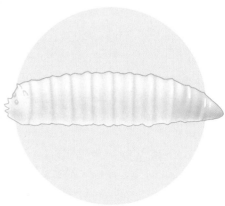

Actual size ¼" long

Damage
No amount of watering will protect cabbage, cauliflower, or other cole crops suffering from wilting caused by cabbage maggot damage.

= range

Adult cabbage maggots are nondescript gray flies, ¼ inch long, with long legs. The white, tapering larvae (which you will probably see much more often than the adult flies) burrow into the roots of plants, where they cause serious damage.

Where They Live
Cabbage maggots are found throughout North America.

Their Life Cycle
In warmer regions, adult flies begin emerging in late March. The females lay eggs in the soil beside the plant roots. After they hatch, the larvae feed on the fine roots, then tunnel into the taproots, feeding for 3

to 4 weeks. They pupate, and adults emerge in 2 to 3 weeks. In most areas, cabbage maggots produce two to four generations a year. The fall generation of pupae overwinters several inches deep in the soil.

Plants They Attack

Cabbage maggots attack all cabbage-family plants.

Why They're a Problem

In the early stages of infestation, plants wilt in the midday heat. Young plants often die, either directly from maggot feeding or because the injured roots become diseased and rot. Older plants may survive but may produce only a small crop. Cabbage-family root crops, such as turnips and radishes, may be ruined. Maggots do the most damage early in the season when the weather is cool and moist. In hot, dry summers, most eggs from later generations never hatch.

Organic Damage Control

- Avoid the most damaging early generation of flies by planting radishes very early.

- Cover seedlings and small plants, such as radishes and Chinese cabbage, with floating row covers, burying the edges under soil well.

- Set out transplants through slits in 6-inch squares of tar paper to prevent flies from laying eggs near stems, or wrap stems with paper 1 to 2 inches above and below the soil line before planting.

- Burn or destroy roots of cabbage-family plants as soon as you harvest the crop.

- Try repelling egg-laying flies by mounding wood ashes, hot pepper, or ginger powder around your plant stems.

quick tip

There are two beneficial insects that can help keep cabbage maggot populations low. **Rove beetles** prey on maggot eggs and young larvae; rove beetle grubs also parasitize the cabbage maggot pupae. **Ground beetles** also feed on cabbage maggots. You can easily attract these beneficial beetles by keeping lots of organic matter in your soil.

COLORADO POTATO BEETLES

Actual size ⅓" long

Damage
Potatoes can usually tolerate light feeding from Colorado potato beetles and their larvae, but large numbers of these pests will defoliate and eventually kill plants.

■ = range

Adults are yellowish orange, with 10 lengthwise black stripes on their wing covers and black spots on their middle section. They are ⅓ inch long. The larvae are dark orange, humpbacked grubs, ranging from ¹⁄₁₆ to ½ inch long. They have a row of black spots along each side. The beetles lay bright yellow eggs on end in upright clusters on the undersides of leaves.

Where They Live

Colorado potato beetles are found throughout most of North America.

Their Life Cycle

In spring, the beetles emerge from the soil to feed on potato plants as soon as the first shoots are up.

After mating, the females lay up to 1,000 eggs each during their several-month life span. The eggs hatch in 4 to 9 days, and the larvae feed for 2 to 3 weeks. They bury into the soil to pupate for another 2 to 3 weeks, and adults emerge in 5 to 10 days. These beetles may produce up to three generations a year. Adults and sometimes pupae overwinter several inches deep in the soil.

Plants They Attack

Colorado potato beetles are major pests of potatoes and, in some areas, damage tomatoes and eggplants, too. They may also attack related plants, such as petunias.

Why They're a Problem

Both adults and larvae chew on leaves and stems of potatoes and related plants. Young plants may die, while older plants can be severely defoliated, which can leave you without any spuds. A moderate amount of feeding, though, doesn't harm plants or reduce yields.

Organic Damage Control

- Choose plant varieties that have some resistance to potato beetles.
- Mulch plants deeply with straw, and trap overwintered beetles in plastic-lined trenches around the potato patch. (The beetles have an easy time crawling or falling into the trench, but they just slip on the plastic when they attempt to crawl back out.)
- Cover susceptible plants with floating row covers until midseason.
- To control larvae, spray *Bacillus thuringiensis* var. *san diego* (BTSD) as soon as eggs are present.
- In the fall, till the soil to kill overwintering beetles.

quick tip

Try planting a trap crop of Chinese lantern plants to thwart Colorado potato beetles. Grow the plants in containers a few feet from your potato patch. (Chinese lanterns spread quickly and can become invasive if not contained.)

CORN EARWORM/TOMATO FRUITWORM

Actual size 1" to 2" long

Damage
Peel back the husk, and you'll find the corn earworm at work.

■ = range

Adults are large, yellowish tan moths with a wingspan of 1½ to 2 inches. The larvae are light yellow, green, pink, or brown caterpillars, 1 to 2 inches long, with white and dark stripes along their sides. Eggs are round and light green, with a ribbed pattern, and are laid singly on undersides of leaves or on corn silks.

Where They Live

This pest is found throughout North America.

Their Life Cycle

Adult moths emerge in early spring in the south to lay eggs, which hatch in 2 to 10 days. Some moths migrate northward, flying long distances before laying eggs later in the season. Caterpillars feed for 2 to 4 weeks, then pupate in the soil. New moths emerge 10 to 25 days later. Pupae overwinter in the soil, although earworm pupae aren't hardy enough to survive the winter in the northern United States and Canada. Corn earworms produce up to four generations a year.

Plants They Attack

Corn, peppers, and tomatoes are the main plants that earworms/fruitworms attack, but the pests have also been reported on beans, cabbage, okra, peanuts, squash, and sunflowers.

Why They're a Problem

The caterpillars feed on fresh corn silks, entering the ear from the tip, then moving down the ear, eating kernels as they go. In tomatoes (which is why they're also called tomato fruitworms), the caterpillars eat the flower buds, chew large holes in leaves, and burrow into ripe fruit. They also chew leaves of other plants.

Organic Damage Control

- Plant corn varieties with tight husks to prevent larvae from entering.
- Attract native parasitic wasps, lacewings, and minute pirate bugs by interplanting with pollen and nectar plants.
- Avoid attracting moths to your garden by keeping nearby lights off at night.
- Inspect plants frequently and handpick caterpillars.
- Apply several drops of vegetable oil to the tip of each ear of corn 3 to 7 days after the silks first appear.

quick tip

If you're having a minor problem with corn earworms, adequate control is easy. Open the cornhusks, and dig out larvae from the tip with a paring knife before they damage the main ear.

CUCUMBER BEETLES

SPOTTED
Actual size ¼" long

STRIPED
Actual size ¼" long

Damage
Cucumber beetles have a voracious appetite for the leaves, flowers, and stems of pumpkin, squash, cucumbers, and melons.

= range

Spotted cucumber beetle adults are greenish yellow, about ¼ inch long, with 12 black spots on their wing covers. The larvae are ¾ inch long, slender, and white with reddish brown heads. **Striped** cucumber beetle adults are yellow, ¼ inch long, with black heads and three wide black stripes on their wing covers. Their larvae look the same as spotted cucumber beetle larvae.

Where They Live

Both types of cucumber beetles are found throughout most of North America.

Their Life Cycle

Spotted cucumber beetles spend the winter under crop debris and clumps of grass, emerging in spring to lay eggs in the soil close to plants (particularly corn). When the eggs hatch, larvae feed in roots of plants for 2 to 4 weeks, then pupate, producing up to three generations a year. (These larvae are a real problem in southern regions, where they're known as corn rootworms.) **Striped** cucumber beetles overwinter in dense grass, emerging from April to early June. Striped cucumber beetles feed on weed pollen for 2 weeks, then lay their eggs. After the eggs hatch, the larvae burrow down to feed on roots for 2 to 6 weeks, after which they pupate. They produce up to four generations a year.

Plants They Attack

These pests eat corn, cucumbers, melons, pumpkins, and squash.

Why They're a Problem

Larvae tunnel into the base of stems and feed on roots, often killing young plants. Adult beetles eat holes in leaves and chew on fruit skin. Cucumber beetles are also thought to transmit bacterial wilt and mosaic viruses, which can cause more damage than the beetles' direct munching.

Organic Damage Control

- Plant wilt- and mosaic-resistant cucumber, squash, and melon varieties to avoid the main damage from these beetles.

- As soon as the seedlings emerge, cover your plants with floating row covers and secure the sides by covering them with soil. When the plants begin to flower, lift the covers for a few hours each morning so bees can pollinate the plants.

- After harvest, pull out and destroy infested spent plants to eliminate overwintering sites.

quick tip

Another great way to foil cucumber beetles is to grow cucumber varieties described as "nonbitter." These varieties, such as 'Marketmore 80', have been bred specifically to be less attractive to cucumber beetles—who like bitterness. (See "Recommended Reading & Resources" on page 99 for more information.)

CUTWORMS

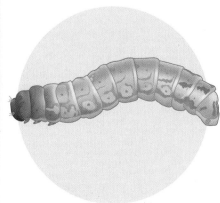

Actual size 1" to 2" long

Damage
If you wake up to find your recently healthy seedling severed at the stem along the soil line, a cutworm is most likely the culprit.

= range

Adult cutworms are large, brownish or gray moths with 1½-inch wingspans. The larvae (which do the damage) are fat, greasy gray or dull brown caterpillars with shiny heads.

Where They Live
You can find cutworms throughout North America.

Their Life Cycle
Adult moths emerge from the overwintering pupae and lay their eggs on grass stems or in the soil from early May to early June. After the eggs hatch (in 5 to 7 days), the cutworms feed on grass and other plants for 3 to 5 weeks, then pupate into the soil. Moths emerge from late August to early September, producing the second generation of the year.

Plants They Attack

These pests attack most early vegetable and flower seedlings, shoots, and transplants.

Why They're a Problem

Cutworm caterpillars feed at night on young plants, usually cutting the stem at or just below the soil line so that the plant topples over. They may completely eat seedlings.

Organic Damage Control

- Protect transplants by putting collars around the stems. You can cut empty paper-towel or toilet-paper rolls into sections to make collars, or use small empty tin cans with the ends removed. Press the collars about 1 inch into the soil.

- Dig around the base of damaged transplants in the morning and destroy hiding larvae.

- Avoid the main population of cutworms by planting later in the season.

A HOME FOR MR. TOAD

TOADS EAT LOTS of pest insects, including cucumber beetles, cutworms, grasshoppers, and slugs. But to attract them to your garden, you'll need to provide shelter for them, as well as garden organically. (The porous skin of a toad is very sensitive and will absorb toxins from chemical sprays.)

Here are some things you can do to make sure that the toads that visit your garden have someplace to call home (or at least a place to hide during the day):

- Use lots of mulch. Toads like to burrow into it.

- Turn a broken clay flowerpot upside down; clay absorbs moisture and stays damp and cool, just the way toads like it.

- Arrange rocks so that there's a hollow space inside.

- Grow a fern grove. Ferns do well in moist, shady spots and their leaves create a great foraging spot for toads while providing protection from predators.

EUROPEAN CORN BORERS

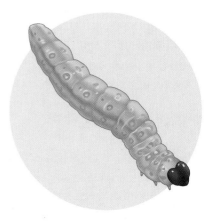

Actual size 1" long

Damage
Newly hatched European corn borers tend to feed inside whorls of young leaves, on corn silks, and inside husks. As they grow larger, they burrow inside the stalks.

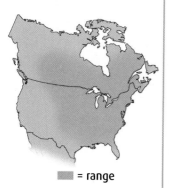

= range

Adult females are pale, yellowish brown moths with 1-inch wingspans. They have dark, zigzag patterns across the wings; male moths are smaller and darker. Larvae are gray or beige, about 1 inch long, with brown heads. They have small brown dots on each segment. Corn borer eggs are white to tan. You'll find them on undersides of leaves in masses of 15 to 20 overlapping eggs.

Where They Live
You'll find European corn borers throughout the Midwest to eastern North America.

Their Life Cycle
Moths generally emerge from dead cornstalks and plant stems (left from last year's garden) in June.

They lay eggs from late June to mid-July. The eggs hatch in a week and the larvae feed for 3 to 4 weeks before spinning a delicate cocoon inside a stalk. The protected cocoons can survive over winter. There are several different strains of corn borers, and they differ in the number of generations a year (from one to three).

Plants They Attack

Corn is the major victim of the borers, and in some regions it is the only vegetable they attack. In other areas, borers may also damage beans, peppers, potatoes, and tomatoes.

Why They're a Problem

Young caterpillars feed on the first whorls of corn leaves, on corn tassels, and beneath the husks of ears. Older larvae burrow into cornstalks and also feed in tassels and ears. Boring weakens stalks, causing them to break easily.

Organic Damage Control

- Start by planting corn varieties with strong stalks and tight husks.

- If you have lots of European corn borers, remove the tassels from two-thirds of your corn plants before the pollen sheds. This eliminates many larvae in the tassels, while leaving enough tassels for pollination.

- Spray *Bacillus thuringiensis* var. *kurstaki* (BTK) twice, a week apart, on leaf undersides and into the tips of corn ears.

- European corn borers overwinter in cornstalks and plant debris, so clean up your corn patch in the fall. Shred and compost the stalks or dispose of them immediately after harvest.

quick tip

You can also combat European corn borers by attracting beneficial insects to your garden, which, in turn, kill the bad borers. Invite tachinid flies (they look a lot like regular houseflies) by planting lots of herbs and then letting them flower. If you can, plant your next corn crop close to some trees, which supply a cool climate for parasitic wasps. Perennials are good to have around, too, as they provide shelter for the wasps when the corn plants are small.

FLEA BEETLES

Actual size ⅒" long

Damage
Flea beetles usually appear in large numbers and chew tiny holes into the leaves of their favorite plants. Heavy infestations can kill young seedlings.

= range

Adult flea beetles are very tiny—just ⅒ inch long. They're black, brown, or bronze with enlarged hind legs. They jump like fleas when they're disturbed. The larvae live in the soil and are thin, white, legless grubs with brown heads.

Where They Live
Flea beetles are found throughout North America.

Their Life Cycle
Adults emerge from the soil in spring to feed and lay eggs on the roots of plants. They die out by early July. The eggs hatch in about a week, and the larvae feed for 2 to 3 weeks. They pupate in the soil, and the next generation of adults emerges in 2 to 3 weeks. These pests

produce up to four generations a year before the final generation of adults settles down for overwintering.

Plants They Attack

Flea beetles attack most vegetables, particularly cabbage-family plants, potatoes, and spinach. They also feed on flowers and weeds.

Why They're a Problem

You can recognize flea beetle damage by the small, round holes the adults chew through leaves. These beetles are most damaging in early spring, when heavy infestations can actually kill seedlings. Larger plants usually survive and outgrow the damage, unless they were infected with a plant virus spread by the beetles. Larvae feed on plant roots.

Organic Damage Control

- Plant susceptible plants as late as possible to avoid the most damaging generation.

- Cover seedlings and potato shoots with floating row covers until adult beetles die off.

- Flea beetles prefer full sun, so interplant crops to shade susceptible plants.

- Lightly cultivate the soil around plants before and after planting to destroy any flea beetle eggs and larvae in the soil.

- Flea beetles like to hide in cool, weedy areas. Prevent them from hopping onto your susceptible crops by surrounding the crops with a 3-foot-wide strip of frequently weeded bare ground.

- Confuse the beetles by mixing up your plantings. Surround their favorite food plants with flowers and herbs like Queen Anne's lace, dill, and parsley, which attract beneficial insects.

quick tip

Some researchers have found that interplanting cabbage with white clover, creeping bentgrass, red fescue, or Kentucky bluegrass reduced the need to control cabbage flea beetles early in the season. Researchers have also found that cabbage flea beetles are slower to find broccoli when it's interplanted with white clover.

IMPORTED CABBAGEWORMS

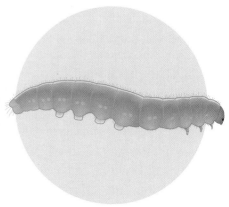

Actual size 1¼" long

Damage
If you notice dark piles of caterpillar droppings (called "frass") on the leaves of cabbage, cauliflower, or broccoli, look for imported cabbageworms hidden nearby.

= range

Adult cabbageworms are the common white butterflies you see in everyone's garden. Their wings are white with black tips and one or two small black spots on the forewing. They have a wingspan of 1½ inches. Cabbageworm larvae are velvety green caterpillars with a fine, light yellow stripe down the back. The eggs are tiny yellow cones laid on undersides of plant leaves.

Where They Live
Imported cabbageworms are found throughout North America.

Their Life Cycle
Adult butterflies emerge in spring to lay eggs on cabbage-family plants. When the eggs hatch, the

caterpillars begin feeding on the undersides of leaves for about 2 to 3 weeks before pupating in garden debris on the soil surface. The butterflies emerge from the pupae in 1 to 2 weeks. Last-generation pupae overwinter in garden debris. These pests produce three to five overlapping generations a year.

Plants They Attack

Imported cabbageworms like to eat nasturtiums, as well as all cabbage-family plants, including broccoli and cauliflower.

Why They're a Problem

Cabbageworm caterpillars bite large, ragged holes in cabbage leaves and chew on cauliflower and broccoli florets. They also soil plants with their dark green droppings and tunnel inside heads of broccoli and cauliflower—where they sometimes go unnoticed until (gulp!) it's too late.

Organic Damage Control

- Plant purple cabbage varieties, which are less often attacked by cabbageworms.
- Cover small plants with floating row covers to prevent butterflies from laying eggs on plants.
- Place yellow sticky traps among host plants to catch female butterflies.
- If you don't have too many caterpillars, try handpicking them.
- If you have a severe cabbageworm infestation, spray *Bacillus thuringiensis* var. *kurstaki* (BTK) at 1- to 2-week intervals.
- Clean up all spent plant debris in the fall and dispose of it in order to thwart cabbageworms the following season.

NATURAL PREDATORS

SPINED SOLDIER BUGS, green lacewings, and syrphid flies all enjoy snacking on the small larvae or eggs of imported cabbageworms. Here are some things you can do to attract each of these good guys.

Spined soldier bugs. Grow pollen-providing plants (adults like to hang out on the flowers of goldenrod, hydrangeas, and milkweed). Maintain undisturbed areas near your garden.

Green lacewings. Grow angelica, caraway, cosmos, dandelion, dill, goldenrod, sunflowers, and sweet alyssum. Provide water in a pan filled with gravel—especially during dry spells—so the delicate insects can alight on the gravel and drink without drowning.

Syrphid flies. Grow pollen and nectar plants, especially sweet alyssum and wild mustard. Allow some broccoli to flower. Landscape with tall plants like sunflowers that break the wind so syrphid flies can hover undisturbed.

JAPANESE BEETLES

Actual size ½" long

Damage
Roses are one of Japanese beetles' favorite foods.

= range

Japanese beetle adults are blocky, metallic blue-green beetles ½ inch long. They have bronze-colored wing covers and their legs are relatively long, with large claws. Beetle larvae are fat, dirty white, C-shaped grubs with brown heads, up to ¾ inch long.

Where They Live
These pests are found throughout the Northeast.

Their Life Cycle
Adult beetles emerge from late June to July. The beetles feed on plants until late summer, then burrow under grasses to lay eggs. The eggs hatch into larvae that feed until cold weather arrives. As fall approaches, the larvae burrow deeper into the

soil to avoid freezing during winter. They move toward the surface again in spring to resume feeding on roots. They pupate in the soil in May and June, so it takes 1 to 2 years for the full life cycle to play itself out.

Plants They Attack

Japanese beetles feed on a variety of vegetables, including beans, corn, and tomatoes, as well as on trees, shrubs, vines, fruits, and flowers. Their larvae damage turfgrass and other grasses.

Why They're a Problem

The beetles chew on flowers and skeletonize leaves, which wilt and drop. If you have lots of beetles, they may completely defoliate plants. Beetle larvae feed on roots of lawn turf and other grasses.

Organic Damage Control

- If you notice a lot of beetles during midsummer, cover smaller or more valuable garden plants with floating row covers.

- In the early morning, handpick beetles or shake them from plants onto sheets, and then drown them in a bucket of soapy water.

- Destroy beetle eggs in your lawn by allowing it to dry out well between waterings in midsummer, or stop watering and allow the grass to go dormant for the summer months.

- Aerate the lawn with spiked sandals to kill grubs while they're close to the soil surface in late spring and early fall.

- Apply parasitic nematodes to the lawn in early spring or early fall when the white grubs are in the soil.

quick tip

Japanese beetle traps not only attract Japanese beetles from your yard, but also from every other yard in the neighborhood. So don't set up traps near your rose bushes. If you really want to use Japanese beetle traps, place the traps at least 50 feet downwind from your plants. That way, you may succeed in luring the beetles *away* from your roses.

LEAFHOPPERS

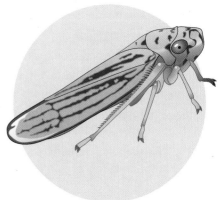

Actual size ¹⁄₁₀" to ½" long

Damage
Leafhoppers secrete a toxic saliva as they feed, causing leaf edges to curl and appear burned.

= range

Adult leafhoppers are mostly wedge-shaped and slender, and range from ¹⁄₁₀ to ½ inch long. Most leafhoppers are either brown or green; some have bright bands of color on their wings. All have well-developed hind legs and can jump rapidly into flight when disturbed. The nymphs are similar to the adults, but paler in color and wingless. They can't fly, but they do hop rapidly when disturbed.

Where They Live
Leafhoppers are found throughout North America.

Their Life Cycle
Female leafhoppers start laying eggs when leaves begin to appear on trees. The eggs hatch in 10 to 14

days and the nymphs develop for 1 to 4 weeks before reaching maturity and laying more eggs. The first fall frosts usually kill any remaining nymphs. Adults usually spend the winter on wild host plants; some species overwinter as eggs. Most species have two to five generations a year.

Plants They Attack

Leafhoppers attack flowers, fruit trees, and vegetables, especially apple trees, beans, eggplant, grapes, peanuts, potatoes, and squash-family plants.

Why They're a Problem

Both adults and nymphs suck juices from stems and undersides of leaves, giving leaves a light, mottled appearance. Their toxic saliva distorts and stunts plants and causes tip burn and yellowed, curled leaves. If you have a lot of leafhoppers, they may stunt the growth of entire plants. Leafhoppers also spread viruses.

Organic Damage Control

- Control nymphs while they're still small by spraying them with insecticidal soap or by washing them from plants with strong sprays of water.

- Cover plants with floating row covers.

- Grow pollen- and nectar-producing plants like goldenrod and yarrow to attract beneficials, such as lady beetles.

- Healthy plants can often tolerate some leafhopper feeding, so keep a watchful eye on susceptible crops and action may not be necessary.

- When possible, grow resistant varieties. For example, certain species of leafhoppers avoid beans and potatoes with fuzzy leaves.

quick tip

The potato leafhopper overwinters only in the Gulf states and has to migrate north every year to do damage. Because it takes a while for potato leafhoppers to get where they're going, their numbers don't peak north of the Gulf states until midsummer. If you live in the North, you can outwit these leafhoppers by planting your potatoes as early as possible and harvesting them by midsummer.

LEAFMINERS

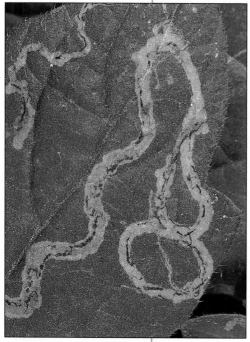

Actual size ⅛" long

Damage
Leafminers leave behind a trail of squiggly lines wherever they go.

■ = range

Leafminers are mostly black or black and yellow flies. They're incredibly small (¹⁄₁₀ inch long), so you've probably never even seen one. Their larvae are pale green, stubby, translucent maggots, found in tunnels between the upper and lower surface of leaves. The eggs are white and cylindrical, and they lay side by side in clusters on leaf undersides.

Where They Live

These pests are found throughout North America.

Their Life Cycle

Adult flies emerge from overwintering cocoons in early spring and lay eggs on leaves. The larvae mine in the leaf tissue for 1 to 3 weeks, then pupate for 2 to 4 weeks. Most species of leafminers have two or three generations a year.

Plants They Attack

Leafminers attack beets, cabbage, chard, lettuce, peas, peppers, spinach, and tomatoes. They're also a problem on trees, ivy, and flowers—especially chrysanthemums and nasturtiums.

Why They're a Problem

Larvae tunnel through leaf tissue and may damage the leaves enough to destroy seedlings. On older plants, though, leafminers are often more of a nuisance than a serious problem. Leafminer damage is also unsightly on ornamentals.

Organic Damage Control

- Cover seedlings with floating row covers to prevent adults from laying eggs.

- Keep row covers on all season on small plants, like beets and chard, where leafminers really like to hang out and eat.

- Remove any nearby dock or lamb's-quarters, which are wild hosts for the beet leafminer.

- In spring, handpick and destroy damaged leaves and egg clusters, which will help reduce later generations.

- Tiny parasitic wasps help to keep leafminer populations under control. Attract these beneficial predators into your garden by making sure that you have lots of flowers blooming throughout the season.

- Keep plants well watered throughout the growing season. Plants suffering from inadequate moisture are more susceptible to leafminer damage.

quick tip

Leafrollers are another pest that wreak havoc on leaves. These green caterpillars with brown or black heads attack mostly fruit crops, spinning webs at branch tips and feeding on the enclosed buds, leaves, and developing fruit. They hatch from eggs laid on bark or leaves by brown moths.

You can control leafrollers by scraping their egg masses from branches in winter. You can also spray dormant oil in late winter to kill eggs. In addition, handpick caterpillars from young trees weekly and handpick the webs and destroy them. Applying *Bacillus thuringiensis* var. *kurstaki* (BTK) to larvae before they spin webs will help control these pests, too.

MEXICAN BEAN BEETLES

Actual size ¼" long

Damage
A hungry hoard of Mexican bean beetles can quickly turn healthy bean leaves into lace.

= range

Adults are oval, yellowish brown to copper-colored beetles, ¼ inch long. They have 16 black spots arranged in three rows across their wing covers and look a lot like lady beetles (which are good guys). The beetle larvae are fat, legless, yellowish orange grubs up to ⅓ inch long. They have six rows of long, branching spines on their body. Eggs are bright yellow ovals laid on end in clusters of 40 to 60 on undersides of leaves.

Where They Live
These pests are found throughout North America, except in the Pacific Northwest.

Their Life Cycle
Adult beetles start to emerge about the time the first bean leaves are up, and more continue to straggle out of hibernation over the next few months. The

beetles feed for a couple of weeks before the females lay eggs on bean plants. After the eggs hatch (in about 5 to 14 days), the larvae feed for 2 to 5 weeks, pupate, and then the beetles emerge about a week later. Mexican bean beetles produce up to four generations a year, with adults overwintering in garden debris or leaf litter.

Plants They Attack

Bean beetles damage all kinds of beans, including cowpeas, lima beans, snap beans, and soybeans.

Why They're a Problem

Larvae and adults skeletonize leaves, leaving behind a characteristic lacy appearance. Attacked plants may produce fewer pods and may be completely defoliated and killed in July and August when beetles are most numerous.

Organic Damage Control

- If you notice Mexican bean beetles in your garden, don't panic. Experts have found that bean plants can tolerate up to 50 percent defoliation and still produce a good crop.
- Plant resistant bean varieties.
- In the South, plant early-season bush beans to avoid damage.
- Cover young plants with floating row covers.
- Leave a few flowering weeds between rows, or interplant your garden with herbs and flowers to attract native predators and parasites.
- Remove or dig in crop debris after harvest to remove overwintering sites.
- Handpick larvae and adults daily.
- Toads love to eat bean beetles. Attract these hungry bug eaters into your garden by providing areas of moist shade.

quick tip

When you're scouting for Mexican bean beetle eggs, start with the lowest leaves, and then move upward. If you see single, not clustered eggs that are pale orange and opaque, leave them alone. They probably belong to the bean beetle's much nicer cousin, the beneficial lady beetle.

PEACHTREE BORERS

Actual size 1¼" long

Damage
Peachtree borers leave behind a trail of sawdust and sticky sap as they bore into trees near the soil line.

= range

These unusual moths have narrow, clear wings with 1¼-inch wingspans. They have a blue-black body, and males have narrow yellow bands around the body. The larvae are white grubs, up to 1 inch long, with dark brown heads.

Where They Live

Peachtree borers are found throughout North America.

Their Life Cycle

Peachtree borers have an unusual life cycle. In July and August, female moths emerge from the soil to lay eggs on trees or soil close to the trunk. The eggs hatch in 12 days and larvae bore under the bark at ground level, where they overwinter before resuming feeding in the roots in spring. The larvae pupate in silken cocoons in the soil by late June or July, usually within a few inches of the trunk.

Plants They Attack

These borers attack mainly peach trees; they also occasionally attack apricot, cherry, nectarine, plum, and prune trees.

Why They're a Problem

Because peachtree borer larvae bore beneath the bark at the base of trees and into the main roots near the surface, they often girdle trees. Their entrance holes are filled with a gum mixed with sawdust. Young or weakened trees may be seriously damaged or killed, whereas older and more vigorous trees that are better established are less likely to be adversely affected.

Organic Damage Control

- Avoid injuries to tree bark from lawn mowers and other pieces of equipment, as adult moths are attracted to injured trees.

- Inspect tree trunks in late summer and remove soil several inches deep around the base of each trunk to look for borer holes containing larvae. Dig out the larvae with a sharp knife or kill them by working a flexible wire into the holes.

- Cultivate the soil shallowly around the trunk to destroy pupae.

- Studies have shown that parasitic nematodes can reduce borer damage by as much as 66 percent. Spray these microscopic beneficials around the trunk of the tree near the soil line in late April. The nematodes will seek out the peachtree borers and parasitize them, releasing a lethal bacteria as they feed.

ORIENTAL FRUIT MOTH

ADULT ORIENTAL fruit moths are small, dark gray moths that lay eggs on fruit trees in spring. Their larvae are white to pinkish gray caterpillars with brown heads. The caterpillars bore into twigs of fruit trees early in the season, causing them to wilt and die. In midsummer, caterpillars bore into developing fruit. Late-summer caterpillars enter the stem end of maturing fruit and bore into the pit.

The larvae overwinter in cocoons on tree bark or in weeds or soil around the trees. They pupate in early spring, and the moths emerge from early May to mid-June to lay eggs.

You can help prevent the oriental fruit moth from getting the better of your fruit trees by planting peach and apricot varieties that bear fruit before midsummer. To destroy overwintering larvae, cultivate the soil 4 inches deep around unmulched trees in early spring. Pick and destroy immature, infested fruit, and spray summer oil to kill eggs and larvae.

SOFT SCALES

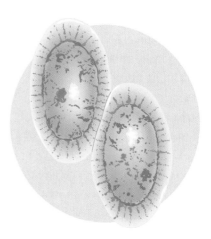

Actual size ¹⁄₁₀" to ¹⁄₅" long

Damage
The leaves on plants suffering from a heavy infestation of soft scale will be covered with the clear sticky honey the insects secrete as they feed.

= range

Female soft scales are tiny oval or round, legless, wingless bumps. Males are minute, yellow-winged insects. The youngest larvae are tiny crawlers resembling minute mealybugs, while older larvae settle and become sedentary.

Where They Live
You'll find scales throughout North America.

Their Life Cycle
Females of some species lay as many as 2,000 eggs, while others give birth to several nymphs per day. Nymphs move around on the plants for a short time, then settle in place to feed. Scales residing outdoors may produce one or two generations a year, while indoor populations may produce up to six generations.

Plants They Attack

Soft scales attack citrus and other fruit trees, as well as ornamental shrubs, trees, and many types of houseplants.

Why They're a Problem

All stages of scales weaken plants and cause leaves to yellow and drop by sucking sap from them. If you have a severe infestation, your plant may die. Soft scales also secrete a sticky substance called honeydew on leaves and fruit as they feed. (Certain species of ants feed on the sticky honeydew—and these ants will actually protect the scale to preserve their food supply.) Sooty mold, a black fungus, grows on the honeydew.

Organic Damage Control

- Attract native parasites and predators to your garden. Tiny parasitic wasps and lady beetles are particularly helpful in controlling scale. So if you have infested houseplants, move them outside for the summer, and let these beneficials clean them up for you.

- Scrub scales gently from twigs with a soft brush and soapy water, or a cloth dipped in insecticidal soap, then rinse well.

- Spray affected plants (including fruit trees) with horticultural oil. (Spray during dormant season when beneficial insects aren't active.)

- Prune and destroy branches and twigs that are significantly infested.

- Wash scale off plants with a strong spray of water from your garden hose. Be sure to hit the undersides of leaves, too.

- Keep your plants healthy. This includes enriching the soil with compost and watering adequately.

SCALES OF ARMOR

ARMORED SCALES are similar to soft scales, except that they are mostly found in the Deep South, Southwest, and California—and they have waxy armor. Adults are tiny round or oval hard bumps, with no visible head or legs. These scales secrete an armor of wax in an oyster shell or circular shape. Depending on the species, they can be ashy gray, yellow, white, reddish, or purplish brown. The early stage nymphs are mobile crawlers, while later stages are legless and hardly move. In the South, armored scales are serious pests of citrus, but they also attack palms, roses, and tropical ornamentals. In the North, they infest fruit and shade trees, currants, grapes, raspberries, and ornamental shrubs. To combat armored scales, apply dormant oil sprays during winter. You can also try summer oil on plants that tolerate it.

SLUGS AND SNAILS

Damage
Slugs and snails chew big holes in leaf margins, sometimes leaving behind a slimy trail in their wake.

■ = range

SLUG
Actual size ⅛" to 1" long

SNAIL
Actual size ⅛" to 1" long

Snails carry coiled shells on their backs, while slugs have no shells. Common species of slugs and snails are ⅛ to 1 inch long. (Banana slugs found in coastal areas stretch from 4 to 6 inches long.) Slugs and snails are gray, tan, green, or black, and some have darker spots or patterns. They leave a characteristic slimy trail of mucus behind. Their eggs are clear, oval, or round and are laid in jellylike masses under stones in the garden.

Where They Live

You'll find these slimers throughout North America.

Their Life Cycle

Adults lay eggs in moist soil, and the eggs hatch in 2 to 4 weeks. Slugs can grow for up to 2 years before reaching maturity.

Plants They Attack

Slugs and snails attack any tender plants, although slugs in particular have a taste for vegetables. Snails can be a serious problem on citrus.

Why They're a Problem

Both slugs and snails feed primarily on decaying plant material. But they also eat soft, tender plant tissue and make large holes in foliage, stems, and even bulbs. They may completely demolish seedlings and severely damage young shoots and plants. They may also crawl up trees and shrubs to feed. Both are most numerous and damaging in wet years and in regions that receive lots of rain.

Organic Damage Control

- Garden organically so that your landscape is a welcome home for many natural enemies of slugs, including birds, garter snakes, toads, and lizards.

- Maintain permanent walkways of clover, sod, or stone mulches to encourage predatory ground beetles.

- Repel slugs and snails with copper strips fastened around trunks of trees or shrubs.

- Edge garden beds with copper flashing or screening (make sure you've removed all the slugs first).

- Protect seedlings temporarily by spreading wide bands of cinders or wood ashes on the soil.

- Set out traps such as pots, boards, or overturned grapefruit rinds; check the undersides of the traps every morning and destroy the slugs you find.

- Bury tin cans with the lip flush to the soil surface and fill the traps with beer to attract slugs. The slugs will fall into the beer and drown.

- Encircle tender young seedlings with a protective barrier of crushed eggshells.

quick tip

If you don't have any beer on hand or don't want to buy any for your tin can slug traps, try filling the traps with slug dough. Mix ½ cup flour, 3 tablespoons of cornmeal, ½ cup water, 1 tablespoon of molasses, and ½ tablespoon of yeast, then fill each tin can with some of the mixture. Check, clean, and rebait the traps with dough every 3 days.

SPIDER MITES

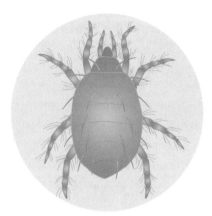

Actual size ¹⁄₇₅" to ¹⁄₅₀" long

Damage
Tiny spider mites feed on plant juices, causing leaves to yellow and drop.

= range

Spider mites are incredibly tiny—less than ¹⁄₇₅ to ¹⁄₅₀ inch long. Adults have eight legs and are reddish, pale green, or yellow and have fine hairs on the body. Some have a darker patch on each side. Most species spin fine webs on plant leaves and shoots. Spider mite eggs are minuscule pearly spheres found on webbing or on leaf hairs.

Where They Live
Spider mites make their homes throughout North America.

Their Life Cycle
Eggs hatch in 1 to 8 days, and nymphs develop into adults in 5 to 10 days. Outdoors, eggs or adults over-

winter in crevices in bark or in garden debris. These pests have a short life cycle and may reproduce year-round on indoor plants.

Plants They Attack

Many vegetables, fruits, and herbs fall prey to spider mites.

Why They're a Problem

Both adults and nymphs suck the juice from plants on the undersides of leaves. If you have a lot of spider mites, their feeding weakens plants, causes leaves to drop, and results in stunted fruit. The first signs of damage are yellowed speckled areas on leaves. In severe infestations, leaves become bronzed or turn yellow or white with brown edges. The webs may cover both sides of the leaves and eventually cover the tips of branches. Spider mite outbreaks can be sudden and severe in hot, dry conditions. When humidity is low, spider mites feed more to avoid drying up, which drives them to lay more eggs, speeding up their development.

Organic Damage Control

- Knock off spider mites with a strong spray of water. Be sure to spray the undersides of leaves, which is where the mites like to feed.
- Maintain high humidity around houseplants and plants in greenhouses.
- Spray dormant oil on fruit trees to kill overwintering spider mite eggs.
- Keep plants well-watered throughout the growing season; moisture-stressed plants are more vulnerable to spider mite attacks.
- Spray infested plants with horticultural oil.

quick tip

Not all mites are bad guys. Predatory mites are invaluable garden helpers. They hang out in trees, shrubs, and surface litter, like fallen leaves and grass clippings. Some species control plant-feeding mites, such as spider mites, while others prey on thrips. In fact, there are many families of soil-dwelling mites that eat insect eggs or decaying organic matter.

SQUASH BUGS

Actual size ½" long

Damage
Leaves begin to droop as squash bugs feed on their juices, then the leaves eventually blacken and die.

= range

Adults are oval, dark brown to black, and very tiny. Their abdomen is flattened and covered with fine, dark hairs. They give off an unpleasant smell in self-defense. The youngest nymphs are pale green, while the older ones are covered with what looks like a grainy gray powder. Squash bug eggs are shiny yellow, turning brick red as they mature, and are laid in groups on the undersides of leaves.

Where They Live
You'll find squash bugs throughout North America.

Their Life Cycle
Female bugs lay eggs in spring. The eggs hatch in 1 to 2 weeks, and the nymphs take 4 to 6 weeks to

develop. Adults overwinter under garden debris, vines, or boards. Squash bugs produce one generation a year.

Plants They Attack

These pests prefer cucumbers, melons, pumpkins, squash, and gourds.

Why They're a Problem

Both adults and nymphs suck plant juices, which causes leaves and shoots to blacken and die. Severely attacked plants may not produce any fruit.

Organic Damage Control

- Plant resistant squash varieties.
- Handpick eggs, nymphs, and adults from the undersides of leaves.
- Support vines off the ground with trellises.
- Place boards on the ground next to plants in early summer and destroy adults found under the boards every morning.
- Tachinid flies will parasitize up to 80 percent of squash bugs in a given area. The flies, which are found throughout most of the United States, lay their eggs on the squash bugs, then their lavae emerge inside the body of the squash bug. Don't kill any squash bugs that you notice carrying little white eggs since the eggs will hatch into more tachinid flies. Attract the adult flies by planting dill, parsley, sweet clover, fennel, buckwheat, goldenrod, wild carrot, or amaranth.
- Remove overwintering sites by cleaning up the garden in fall.
- Protect young seedlings with row covers until the plants are large enough to sustain some damage and still produce a crop.

SQUASH VINE BORERS

ANOTHER PEST that attacks squash family plants is the squash vine borer, which is found throughout North America (except for the West Coast). Adults, which are narrow-winged, olive brown moths, lay eggs on stems near the bases of plants. The larvae are white grubs with a brown head and bore into squash vines. The vines wilt suddenly, and girdled vines rot and die. The larvae may also feed on fruit later in the season.

Squash vine borer larvae or pupae overwinter in the soil. Adults emerge as squash vines begin to lengthen and then lay their eggs on stems and leaf stalks. The larvae burrow into stems for 4 to 6 weeks, then pupate in the soil for winter. These pests usually produce only one generation a year.

Control borers by planting early or late to avoid the main egg-laying period. Also fertilize plants to promote vigorous growth so the vines are better able to tolerate borer attacks.

TARNISHED PLANT BUGS

Actual size ¼" long

Damage
Tarnished plant bugs feed on hundreds of different kinds of plants, causing blackened shoots, misshapen fruit, and dropped or damaged flowers.

= range

Tarnished plant bug adults are quick-moving, oval bugs that are ¼ inch long. They're a mottled light green to coppery brown and their top wings have a black-tipped yellow triangle on each side. Nymphs are yellowish green with five black dots on the body, similar to adult bugs, but wingless. Tarnished plant bugs lay their eggs into plant stems or leaves.

Where They Live
These bugs make their homes throughout North America.

Their Life Cycle
Adults emerge in early spring to feed on fruit buds and other early foliage. They move to garden plants

or weeds, such as clover, chickweeds, and dandelions, to lay eggs. The eggs hatch in 10 days; nymphs feed for about 3 weeks, then molt to adults. Tarnished plant bugs produce up to five overlapping generations a year; the adults overwinter under fallen leaves.

Plants They Attack

Most flowers, fruits, vegetables, and weeds are food for tarnished plant bugs.

Why They're a Problem

Both adults and nymphs suck the juice from leaves, buds, and fruit. Their toxic saliva causes buds and pods to drop and distorts leaves and shoots. Parts of plants wilt or are stunted, and branch tips blacken and die back. Feeding on tomatoes and other fruit causes pitted catfacing on the fruit, while feeding on broccoli and cauliflower leaves dead spots on florets.

Organic Damage Control

- Cover plants with floating row covers, especially if you have a lot of tarnished plant bugs.

- Keep your garden free of weeds and dead plant debris, and make sure to remove spent plants at the end of the season.

- Grow pollen and nectar plants, such as sweet alyssum, daisies, and cosmos, to attract native predatory bugs such as big-eyed bugs and minute pirate bugs, which feed on nymphs.

- In vegetable gardens, plant cool-season cover crops like subterranean clover. These cover crops attract big-eyed bugs, one of tarnished plant bugs' natural enemies.

quick tip

Damsel bugs are another predator of tarnished plant bugs. You can use a butterfly net to collect damsel bugs from alfalfa, cotton, and soybean fields with a butterfly net and then release them into your own garden.

THRIPS

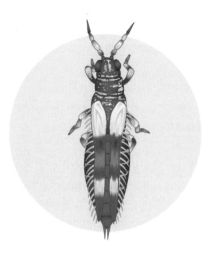

Actual size ¹⁄₅₀" to ¹⁄₂₅" long

Damage
Another insect that feeds on plant juices, thrips will stunt plant growth and cause fruit and flowers to become distorted.

= range

Adult thrips are minute—about ¹⁄₅₀ to ¹⁄₂₅ inch long. They're yellowish brown or black and have narrow, fringed wings. They move quickly and like to hide in tight crevices in plant stems and flowers. Nymphs are light green or yellow and look similar to adults, but smaller.

Where They Live
You'll find thrips throughout North America.

Their Life Cycle
Adults become active in early spring and lay eggs in plant tissue. The eggs hatch in 3 to 5 days, and the nymphs feed for 1 to 3 weeks before molting to the adult stage. Thrips produce many generations a year

and breed year-round in greenhouses; adults over-winter in sod, debris, or cracks in bark.

Plants They Attack

These bad bugs attack asparagus, cabbage, lettuce, onions, peas, flowers, and fruit and shade trees.

Why They're a Problem

Both adults and nymphs suck the contents of plant cells. In severe infestations, they leave plants stunted and distorted and flowers damaged. Some species spread tomato spotted wilt virus.

Organic Damage Control

- Plant pollen and nectar plants and provide a water source in your garden to attract predators such as lacewings and lady beetles.
- Spray dormant oil in early spring to control thrips attacking fruit trees.
- Use bright blue or yellow sticky traps to catch adults in greenhouses.
- Wash thrips off with a strong spray of water from your garden hose.

quick tip

Instead of buying commercial sticky coating to spread on your homemade sticky traps, try using axle grease, which is less expensive. Or mix equal parts petroleum jelly or mineral oil and liquid dish soap.

DISCOVER THE WORLD'S SAFEST INSECTICIDE: WATER!

IT MAY BE tempting to bring out the arsenal when you find your favorite rosebush infested with aphids, but a safer and less-expensive solution is as close as the end of your hose—water! Researchers at Texas A&M University have been able to knock out 70 to 90 percent of aphid infestations by spraying water through a specially designed hose. A strong shot of water will wash away spider mites and thrips, too! You don't necessarily need a high-tech wand on the end of your hose, though; you can achieve good results using an ordinary watering wand. Just make sure to spray both the upper and lower sections of the leaves. Once those pests hit the ground, it's very difficult for them to make it back onto your plants.

WHITEFLIES

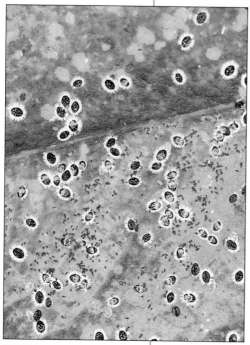

Actual size ¹⁄₂₀" long

Damage
Snowy clouds of whiteflies emerge from infested plants when you brush against them.

= range

Adult whiteflies are tiny, powdery-white insects, $\frac{1}{20}$ inch long. Although their name suggests that they're related to flies, they really aren't—they're related to aphids. Whiteflies rest on the undersides of leaves and fly up when they're disturbed. Nymphs are tiny, flattened, translucent scale also found on the undersides of leaves. The eggs are gray or yellow cones the size of a pinpoint.

Where They Live

Whiteflies are a pest throughout North America.

Their Life Cycle

The complete whitefly life cycle takes only 20 to 30 days at room temperature. The eggs hatch in 2 days into tiny scales; the scales feed on plant juices before molting to adults. These bugs produce many overlapping generations a year, continuing all winter in greenhouses and warm climates. In cold winter areas, whiteflies can't survive outdoors in winter. However, they can reinfest gardens each spring if they're brought in on infested transplants from commercial greenhouses and nurseries.

Plants They Attack

Whiteflies attack citrus plants and many vegetable crops, especially squash and tomato family plants.

Why They're a Problem

Both nymphs and adults suck plant juices, weakening plants. They can spread plant viruses through their feeding. They also exude honeydew, which supports the growth of sooty molds on leaves and fruit.

Organic Damage Control

- Capture adult whiteflies on yellow sticky traps.
- Use a handheld vacuum to suck up adults from the undersides of leaves (you can do this if the infestation isn't too severe).
- Control nymphs with insecticidal soap.
- Wash the sticky coating from leaves with water.
- Smother whiteflies with a spray of horticultural oil. Spray during the cool times of the day since the oil can react with sunlight and damage plant leaves.
- Attract wasps that parasitize whiteflies into your garden by providing food and shelter. Parasitic wasps feed on the nectar of parsley, dill, Queen-Anne's lace, daisies, sunflowers, and coneflowers. Grow tall plants like corn and sunflowers to protect these tiny fliers from the wind.

quick tip

Another effective control for whiteflies, particularly the sweet potato whitefly, is to allow 2 weeks between crops. After you harvest one crop, clean up all the spent plant debris, then wait 2 weeks before planting your next crop. Whiteflies have nothing to feed on during those 2 weeks and will either die off or move on.

You can keep animal pests, such as this sweet-looking fawn, from snacking on your garden. You just need to tailor your control to the specific critter.

chapter five

Animal Pests

Although Bambi, Peter Rabbit, and other four-footed creatures may look awfully cute, they can cause more damage than insects in many gardens. Hungry animal pests can plow their way through everything from apples to zinnias. You can beat animal pests at their own game, however, without resorting to traps. You simply need to know how to outsmart them.

DEER

These innocent-looking animals can be either a gentle nuisance or downright detrimental to your plantings, depending on how many of them are in your neighborhood. Deer feed mostly at dawn and dusk, nibbling on foliage in a way that leaves a distinctive jagged edge. You're also likely to encounter deer droppings in the area of deer damage, as well as a wealth of distinctive two-toed tracks.

Greatest Cravings

Deer love corn, most vegetables, fruit trees (leaves, flowers, and bark), shrubbery, and flowers—especially roses. Keep in mind, though, that a deer's preference will vary according to what's available. So when they're hard-pressed for a meal, they'll devour nearly any edible plants.

Critter Control

Fences. Installing an electric fence is the most effective way to keep deer out, but that probably isn't practical for many home gardeners. Conventional fences should be 8 feet high for best protection. A second fence about 3 feet high placed outside the first one will increase effectiveness because double

When deer are hard-pressed for a meal, they'll devour nearly any edible plants.

YOUR BEST DEFENSE

YOUR BEST DEFENSE against deer is not a conventional fence, but an electric one. You might want to try a single strand of electrically charged wire strung 2½ feet high. Wrap strips of masking tape at 3-foot intervals along the fence and then smear the tape with peanut butter. Cover the peanut butter bait with flaps of aluminum foil to make it more noticeable to deer (and to protect it from being quickly gobbled up). When Bambi ambles up to get a nibble, she'll get a little zap—which should be enough of a deterrent to keep her out of your garden.

If you install electric fencing yourself, be sure you understand and follow all of the manufacturer's safety instructions, or else have a professional install it for you.

obstacles confuse deer. They're also not likely to jump a high, solid fence, such as one made of stone or wood.

Barriers. If deer are damaging a few select trees or shrubs, encircle the plants with 4-foot-high cages made from galvanized hardware cloth. The hardware cloth should be several feet away from the plants so the hungry deer can't reach over and nibble.

Repellents. For minor deer-damage problems, repellents may be effective. Buy soap bars in bulk and hang them from strings in trees—or hang nylon stockings filled with hair (human, cat, or dog) around vulnerable plants. Spray plants with a mixture of two or three rotten eggs blended in a gallon of water, or 2 tablespoons of hot pepper sauce per gallon of water. (Spray plants thoroughly and make sure to reapply after rain.)

A 4-foot-high cage of galvanized hardware cloth can protect shrubs from nibbling deer.

RABBITS

Rabbits can damage vegetables, flowers, and trees at any time of year in any setting. They're most active early in the morning and late afternoon and will nibble plants clear down to ground level.

Greatest Cravings

These furry fellows relish beans, beets, carrots, lettuce, peas, and strawberries during the gardening season, and the bark of fruit bushes and trees (apple, blackberry, raspberry, etc.) in the winter. They generally don't eat corn, cucumbers, peppers, potatoes, squash, or tomatoes.

Keep rabbits out of your plants with a chicken-wire fence—or get a dog for bunny control.

Critter Control

Fences. The best way to keep rabbits out of a garden is to erect a chicken-wire fence, of which at least 6 inches is buried in the ground. Be sure the mesh is 1 inch or smaller so that young rabbits can't squeeze through.

Barriers. To guard fruit trees and canes against ravenous rabbits in winter, wrap their trunks (or in the case of canes, the entire plant) with hardware cloth, burlap, plastic or aluminum foil extending at least 18 inches above the highest snowfall you might expect. (Rabbits' paws are the original snowshoes.)

Other methods. Spread ground black pepper, chili powder, bloodmeal, rotten eggs, or hot sauce around your plants. Inflatable snakes may scare rabbits away as will a dog if you happen to own one. And remove any piles of debris or brush from around your garden; they can serve as between-meal hideouts.

MOLES AND GOPHERS

BOTH MOLES AND GOPHERS burrow in the ground, creating extensive tunnels. In some ways, **moles** are gardeners' allies. That's because moles aerate soil and eat insects, including many plant pests. However, they also eat earthworms—and their tunnels can be an annoyance. Plus, other small animals also may use the tunnels and eat the plants that moles leave behind. To prevent moles from invading an area, dig a trench about 6 inches wide and 2 feet deep around the perimeter. Fill it with stones or dried, compact material such as crushed shells, then cover the material with a layer of soil.

Gophers eat mostly root vegetables and flower bulbs. They also feed on the root systems of shrubs (and have been known to chew on underground cables as well).

You can help keep gophers out of your beds by burying ¼- to ½-inch wire mesh so that it extends 2 feet below and 2 feet above the soil surface around your garden.

MICE AND VOLES

Mice and voles look alike and cause similar damage, but they are only distantly related. These little guys are active at all times of day, year-round (meaning your garden is always fair game).

Greatest Cravings

Mice and voles eat almost any green vegetation, including tubers and bulbs. When they can't find other foods, they'll eat the bark and roots of fruit trees. They can severely damage young apple trees.

Critter Control

Barriers. Sink cylinders of wire mesh or ¼-inch hardware cloth several inches into the soil around the base of trees.

Other methods. Repellents such as those described for deer and rabbits may control damage. You can also discourage mice and voles by removing mulch around trees in fall and mowing thick grass to reduce cover for them to hide in.

Discourage mice from hanging out around your yard by removing mulch around trees in fall.

GROUNDHOGS

Groundhogs (or woodchucks, as they're also known) are large, lumbering, rodentlike animals. You're most likely to see them in the early morning or late afternoon, munching on a variety of green vegetation. Because groundhogs hibernate during winter, they're likely to be their most pesky in early spring, eating the young plants in your garden.

Groundhogs love young plants, so give your transplants or newly sprouted charges protection with floating row covers.

Greatest Cravings

These four-legged foes will devour nearly any vegetation in their path and usually with the worst of table manners, uprooting plants and eating them only partially before moving on to something else. Beans, lettuce, melons, peas, and squash are especially attractive fare for groundhogs. (Corn is not normally a groundhog favorite.)

Critter Control

Fences. Groundhogs can climb almost as nearly as well as they can dig, so if you put up a fence (chicken wire works well), you should bury it at least 10 to 12 inches deep. You should also create a floppy baffle of at least 12 to 18 inches of wire at the top of the fence to discourage a groundhog from climbing up and over the fence.

Barriers. Cover young plants with clear plastic or floating row covers (make sure to remove them when the plants are ready for pollination).

Repellents. Groundhogs don't like spicy food, so sprinkling some dried, ground-up hot peppers or regular old black pepper in the vicinity of their favorite dishes will sometimes dull their appetites.

quick tip

Although Mr. Raccoon may look cute, he's still a wild animal—and that means you should keep your distance. Wild animals are unpredictable and may bite or scratch. And, in doing so, they can transmit serious diseases such as rabies. If you're planning to catch animal pests in live traps, be sure you've planned a safe way to transport and release the animals *before* you set out the traps.

RACCOONS

These masked bandits prefer to pillage at night. They will go through not only your gardens but your compost heap and garbage cans as well.

Greatest Cravings

Raccoons love corn and will strip ears clean. Other signs that they have dined include broken stalks, shredded husks, scattered kernels, and gnawed cob ends. They also like melons and will bore small holes in these fruits and scoop the insides clean.

Critter Control

Fences. Installing an electric fence is the best way to prevent raccoon damage, although that may not be practical for home gardeners. If you decide to pursue an electric fence, you'll need two strands of wire—one at 6 inches and the other at 12 inches above the ground. You'll also need to use fiberglass posts because raccoons can climb wooden ones without any trouble. (Again, your best bet is to have a professional install the fence for you.)

Habitat modification. Lighting the garden at night may work as a deterrent. Or try planting squash among the corn—the prickly foliage may keep coons at bay.

Barriers. Protect small corn plantings by wrapping ears at the top and bottom with strong tape. Loop the tape around the tip of the ear, then around the stalk, then around the base of each ear. This prevents raccoons from pulling the ears off the plants. Or, try covering each ear with a paper bag secured with a rubber band.

Planting squash around corn may help keep raccoons from feasting on your kernels.

THE BIRDS

BIRDS CAN BE BOTH friends and foes in your garden. While they eat insect pests, many birds also pick at your produce, leaving damage that invites disease and spoils your harvest. One of the things you can do to eliminate pesky birds is to change the garden environment, such as removing garden trash and covering possible perches to discourage smaller flocking birds (like sparrows and finches) that often post a guard. You can also cover shrubs and trees with plastic netting, and cover vegetables with floating row covers.

Using scare tactics is another way to deal with pesky birds. You can scare birds by fooling them into thinking their enemies are present by using one or more of the following techniques:

- Place inflatable, solid, or silhouetted likenesses of snakes, hawks, or owls strategically around your garden. (They'll be most effective if you occasionally reposition them so that they appear to move about the garden.) Kites and mylar balloons that will move in the breeze and mimic predators will startle birds.

- Put up a humming line—a line made of thin nylon (fishing line works well) that vibrates in the slightest breeze. The movement creates humming noises inaudible to us but readily heard and avoided by birds. Or, string up aluminum pie plates on stakes in and around your garden.

- Use that tried-and-true method—make a scarecrow.

Bad bugs aren't to blame for everything. Drastic changes in temperature, for example, can also cause plant problems.

chapter six

Pest Imposters

Although bad bugs can cause their fair share of plant problems, they can't be the fall guys for everything. Brown patches on leaves, stunted growth, or odd-looking spots, for example, aren't necessarily the work of a pest. Rather, they might be the result of drastic changes in temperature or of disease. In this chapter, you'll learn about seven pest imposters and how you can control them (organically, of course).

WINTER INJURY

If you wake up one morning to discover that your prize rhododendrons have taken a turn for the worse, the problem may not be pests, but the weather instead. Sudden or abnormally cold winter temperatures can cause plant tissues to die, leaving your plants looking less than stellar.

The symptoms of winter injury appear different depending on what type of plant is affected. For example, large brown patches may appear on broad-leaved evergreens such as rhododendrons, and tip or shoot dieback can be seen on woody perennials, including those with needles. You may also notice that some of your plants have brown, dry branches on only one side.

So what plants are susceptible to winter damage? Most plants, particularly those that are only marginally hardy for a growing region and those with shallow root systems.

Another type of winter injury to plants results from alternating freezing and thawing. This can cause roots to heave out of the soil, leaving them vulnerable to cold temperatures and drying winds. Rhododendrons, roses, and strawberries are all extremely susceptible to winter heaving.

Sudden cold winter temperatures can leave your plants looking less than stellar.

Organic Controls

- Choose plant varieties that are reliable in your hardiness zone. (If you're not sure what zone you live in, call your local Cooperative Extension office.)

- Water perennials thoroughly through late summer and early fall.

- Protect tree trunks with a thorough coating of white latex paint.

- Mulch perennials with 6 inches of straw or another organic mulch after the top surface of the soil has frozen.

- Create a windbreak in windy areas with stakes and burlap, or wrap susceptible shrubs in burlap for the winter.

SALT INJURY

TOO MUCH SALT in the soil can wreak havoc on almost all plants. If you garden organically and live in a rainy climate, the main source of salt in your soil is usually the de-icing material used on roads and sidewalks in winter. However, if you live in the West, your soil or water might be naturally salty. If you live on the coast, windblown salt spray can add to salt injury.

Too much salt is a bad thing for plants because it damages the roots or prevents them from taking in enough nutrients. Plants that are victims of salt injury will wilt when the soil is moist and have yellowing and dying leaves; also, their growth will be stunted. In coastal areas or near heavily salted roads, vulnerable plants usually show scorching around the outsides of the leaves first. Leaf wilting, yellowing, and dying follow.

To prevent salt damage, choose salt-tolerant plants such as yews in arid and coastal regions as well as in areas that get lots of runoff. If salts are building up in your soil because of poor drainage, add compost to improve the soil structure.

Yellowing of plant leaves is indicative of salt injury.

- Check roots of perennials for heaving in spring when the soil begins to thaw, and rebury any that need it.

- Carefully prune out all injured branches.

SUNSCALD

Sunscald is the result of a sudden exposure to sunlight and is most damaging to tree bark, seedlings, and the fruits of apples, grapes, peppers, and tomatoes. Splits or cracks may appear in tree bark when warm conditions start heating things up but the ground is still frozen, preventing roots from taking up water. Injured seedlings that have minor sunscald damage can lose their leaves; in severe cases, the stems wither and die. On fruit, sunscald injuries initially look like water-soaked blisters on the skin. These areas eventually become dried, brown, and sunken, often surrounded by a grayish white margin.

The blisterlike patch on this pepper is a telltale sign of sunscald.

Sunscald in tree bark is caused by bright light and warm temperatures during the winter, particularly when there's a reflective layer of snow on the ground. Sudden exposure to bright light can injure or kill seedlings. Fruits develop sunscald if sheltering leaves drop or are pruned off the plant.

Organic Controls

- Prevent injury to tree trunks by painting them with white latex paint or wrapping them with vented, light-reflective covering.

- Gradually harden off seedlings for at least a week before transplanting them outside or exposing them to a full day of sunlight.

- Choose disease-resistant fruit varieties to avoid summer leaf loss. Also avoid excessive summer pruning of plants.

- Tape or clip shade cloths over developing grape clusters to protect them from the sun's rays.

WATERLOGGED SOIL

Although water is essential for growing plants, too much of it can actually be a bad thing. And too much water—whether it comes in the form of lots of rain, poor drainage, or overwatering—can lead to waterlogged soil. That, in turn, can be the downfall (i.e., death) of your prized plants.

When soil has too much water in it, all of the soil's pore spaces fill with water, leaving plant roots without any access to oxygen. If the water subsides fairly quickly, plants can usually recover. However, in instances where waterlogged soil persists, plant roots die and become an easy target for fungi and bacteria.

Too much rain or poor drainage can mean disease or death for plant roots.

Organic Controls

- Don't overwater your plants; water often enough so that the soil is consistently moist, but not so much that it's soggy.

- Increase drainage in container plants by using a well-aerated soil mix.

- Add compost, gypsum, or greensand to beds with poor drainage.

- Build raised beds in areas with poor drainage.

BLOSSOM END ROT

Blossom end rot is a symptom of calcium deficiency in plants and particularly affects tomatoes and peppers. If your plants have blossom end rot, you'll notice a dark-colored, watery spot on the blossom end of the fruit. This area enlarges and the skin sometimes becomes brown and leathery. Often, it dries and wrinkles over the dark, sunken area below it. The damaged patch of tissue provides an easy entry for pests and disease.

Blossom end rot can occur when sunny days follow a cloudy, wet period. Because calcium moves slowly in plants, deficiencies can occur even if a soil test shows you have adequate calcium in your soil. Drought can contribute to blossom end rot as can extremely rapid growth in plants because the slow-moving calcium can't move into tissues quickly enough.

This dark-colored spot on the blossom end of this tomato is a sign of blossom end rot.

Organic Controls

- Water during dry periods to prevent changes in soil moisture, especially if you live where summer rain is irregular.

- Mulch deeply with straw or rotted hay.

- Fertilize plants with finished compost, and don't add extra nitrogen unless you absolutely need to.

- Have your soil tested every few years and correct any imbalances.

EARLY BLIGHT

Early blight is a fungal disease that affects all tomato-family crops, particularly tomatoes and potatoes. The first signs of early blight are brown leaf spots with a concentric target pattern. The spots can be as large as ½ inch in diameter; over time they run together. Leaves that are heavily infected with early blight drop, and dark sunken lesions appear on the stems, often starting near the soil in young plants.

Early blight infections on tomatoes start at the stem ends and form a dark-colored rot inside the fruit. Blight damage to potatoes looks like small, dark spots, often with gray or purplish edges.

This disease overwinters on seeds and crop debris left in the garden. In spring, spores form as soon as the weather begins to warm. The spores are spread by factors such as wind, rain, and contaminated tools.

Because early blight overwinters on plant debris left in the garden, you should try to clean up spent plants at the end of the season.

Organic Controls

- Provide good plant care, since stressed plants are more susceptible to early blight.

- Rotate your garden crops.

- Clean up all garden debris in fall.

- Destroy any severely infected plants.

- Mound soil over potato tubers to prevent infection.

VERTICILLIUM WILT

Tomato plants with lower leaves that wilt even in moist soil may be suffering from a fungal disease with a fancy name: verticillium wilt. If verticillium wilt is the problem, those leaves may proceed to turn yellow, then brown, and finally drop off the plant.

The leaves on a healthy tomato plant (top) are lush and full compared to those affected by verticillium wilt (bottom).

Verticillium wilt is an extremely common disease. It affects many plants, especially tomato- and squash-family crops, asters, chrysanthemums, small fruits, and ornamental shrubs. The symptoms may look different from one kind of plant to another. For example, on chrysanthemums, the wilting leaves may develop a pinkish color.

Verticillium fungi overwinter in crop debris; in spring, when the weather gets warmer and the soil is moist, spores germinate. The fungus enters plants through natural openings in roots and through plant wounds.

Organic Controls

- Choose resistant pepper and tomato varieties.
- Plant in well-drained soil that warms quickly.
- Remove all crop debris and compost it in hot piles.
- Rotate vegetable crops on a 4-year schedule.

Your Seasonal Pest-Fighting Calendar

NOW YOU'VE learned all about the different types of insect and animal pests that might visit your garden and how to control them. Here's what you should be doing each month of the year to help protect your garden from these creatures and critters.

That's where this handy calendar comes in. It lists helpful hints that you can use even during the months when you're not growing anything in your beds—so that you get the better of pests, and not the other way around.

JANUARY

Winter isn't too early to start thinking about pest control. You can:

- **Figure out a rotation plan** for your vegetable beds so that you're not growing the same plant family in the same location each year.

- **Make a list of pollen- and nectar-providing plants,** such as alyssum and goldenrod, that you can incorporate into your beds to attract beneficials.

- **Research what pest problems** are common in your area and how you can control them organically.

FEBRUARY

Finalize what you want to plant this year. If you're **buying seeds** or plants through mail-order catalogs, try to choose varieties **with resistance to pests** that are common in your area. Consider fencing your garden if you have a serious problem with groundhogs and rabbits.

MARCH

With warmer weather just around the corner, now is the time to:

- **Check out** the condition of **your garden soil;** healthy plants are much less likely to be attacked by pests.

- **Add compost to your beds,** and make sure they have good drainage.

- **Choose appropriate sites** for your plants (for example, make sure shade lovers aren't growing in full sun) to give them the opportunity to thrive.

- **Put up birdhouses** and bat houses around your property to encourage these pest-eating creatures.

- **Prune diseased wood** out of fruit trees and shrubs to make them less inviting homes to pests.

APRIL

Mulch garden beds with grass, hay, wood chips, or other organic materials **to suppress weeds.** Begin patrolling your garden to learn what pests and beneficials are residing there. Give that cracked clay flowerpot a second life as a **toad house** in your garden. Inspect any plants you buy to make sure they're free of insects.

MAY

Put **row covers** on seedlings after you plant them to **prevent insect pest damage,** such as flea beetles on eggplant and cabbage loopers on broccoli and cabbage. Sink shallow **dishes of beer** into the soil around your beds to lure slugs to their demise.

Winter

Spring

Summer

Fall

JUNE

Although you may take vacation time during summer, pests stay hard at work. So this month:

- **Time your vegetable plantings** to avoid the worst pests.
- **Watch for aphid colonies** on lush young growth, and use a heavy stream of water or a soap spray to reduce their populations.
- **Handpick** pest insects.
- **Pick up damaged fruit** off the ground so it's not inviting to insect and animal pests.
- **Use a summer oil spray** if spider mites, scale, or mealybugs are a big problem on trees and shrubs.

JULY

Your garden is in full swing now, producing juicy tomatoes and luscious peppers—inviting snacks for insect and animal pests. Remember to:

- **Continue patrolling** your garden and hand-picking insect pests.
- **Spread ground black pepper** or chili powder around your beds to repel hungry rabbits. If you have a **dog,** let him police your garden to help scare rabbits away.
- **Hang old nylon stockings** filled with cat or dog hair around plants that deer like to eat.

AUGUST

Continue to patrol the garden for pest problems and **pull out weeds** and diseased plants. Enjoy the harvest as summer starts to fade away.

SEPTEMBER

Take notes on which **varieties did well** in your garden and which were prone to pest problems. Also **make notes** on which beneficials visited your garden; that way, you can be sure to grow plants next year that will attract them.

OCTOBER

Remove mulch from around the base of fruit trees to **discourage mice** from nesting there and nibbling on root systems. Put hardware cloth tree guards around young trees to prevent mice and rabbits from eating the bark.

NOVEMBER

Now that the growing season is pretty much over, it's time to ready your garden for winter.

- **Clean up** any remaining spent **vegetable plants** for the winter and compost the debris (except for diseased plants, which you should dispose of).
- Be sure to **leave spent perennials** in your beds so overwintering beneficials will have someplace to live during the cold months.
- **Mulch perennial and strawberry beds** with a layer of straw to prevent winter injury.

DECEMBER

Hang strong-scented soap bars in trees and shrubs to deter deer. Put up feeders for your feathered friends. **Relax** by the fire with a good book, and **dream** about warmer days ahead.

Pest Glossary

Learning the lingo that goes with fighting pests will make your trips to the home or garden center easier. Here's a list of terms you're likely to come across in this book as well as in the gardening aisles of your favorite home or garden center.

Abdomen. The last section of an insect's body, following the head and thorax. Digestive and reproductive organs are found in the abdomen.

Antenna. Paired, segmented structures, also called feelers. One on each side of the head. Aid sensory perception. Plural antennae.

Bacteria. A single-celled microorganism that reproduces by simple cell division. Beneficial bacteria can help control insect pests, but some bacteria species can cause serious plant diseases, like bacterial wilt and fire blight.

Beak. Long mouthpart used by sucking insects to pierce the surface of a plant or animal. Hollow and jointed. One or more tiny needles in the beak pierce the tissue.

Beneficials. Helpful creatures—birds, bats, toads, snakes, spiders, and predatory insects—that eat garden pests.

Biological controls. Pest-control measures that use living organisms to fight other living organisms. Examples include releasing and attracting natural insect predators and parasites and using microbial sprays to control insects and diseases.

BT. *Bacillus thuringiensis*. A spray derived from naturally occurring bacteria that kill certain insect larvae.

BTK. A BT variety (*B. thuringiensis* var. *kurstaki*) that controls cabbage loopers, cabbageworms, tomato hornworms, fruitworms, European corn borers, and pest larvae.

Caterpillar. Larval stage of a butterfly or moth. Segmented or wormlike, with a distinct head, 12 simple eyes, a pair of very short antennae, and usually six well-developed legs, as well as two to five pairs of prolegs.

Chrysalis. The tubular, hard pupal shell of a butterfly.

Cocoon. The silken pupal case of a butterfly or moth.

Companion planting. Combinations of plants that work well together to repel pests, attract beneficial insects, or make efficient use of garden bed space.

Compost. Decomposed and partially decomposed organic matter (such as kitchen scraps, leaves, grass clippings, dead plants) that is dark in color and crumbly in texture. Used as an amendment, compost increases the water-holding capacity of the soil and is an excellent nutrient source for microorganisms, which later release nutrients to your plants.

Composting. The art and science of combining organic material so that the original raw ingredients are transformed into compost.

Compost tea. A fertilizer made by soaking a cloth bag full of compost in a watering can or barrel for several days.

Compound eye. Eye of an insect, composed of separate, close-fitting hexagonal lenses. Sensitive to movement and color. Larvae lack compound eyes.

Crop rotation. Rotating crops from different botanical families to avoid or reduce problems with soilborne diseases or soil insects.

Cultural controls. These are gardening practices that reduce pest problems and include building organically enriched, biologically active soil, selecting well-adapted disease-resistant varieties, keeping the garden clean, and practicing crop rotation.

Dormant. Inactive; in suspended animation; hibernating. Dormancy occurs in winter.

Dormant oil. A heavy petroleum oil that can be sprayed on dormant orchard trees and ornamental plants to control overwintering stages of mites, scales, aphids, and other insects. See also Summer oil.

Exoskeleton. The hard outer covering or skeleton that protects an insect's body like armor. Forms a jointed frame.

Frass. The sawdustlike excrement of borers, such as the peachtree borer and squash vine borer.

Fungi. A generally beneficial spore-producing organism that helps the decomposition process. Fungi also cause many common plant diseases such as powdery mildew and late blight.

Grub. The larva of a beetle. Grubs are plump, flat, or wormlike, with well-developed heads and 3 pairs of legs. They pupate in the soil or other protected sites.

Hibernation. A winter period of suspended animation passed by many insects that live more than one season. Usually spent in soil or garden debris.

Honeydew. A sweet, sticky substance secreted by aphids as they feed. Honeydew allows sooty mold to grow on leaves.

Horticultural oils. See Dormant oil; Summer oil.

Host. A plant or animal that a parasite or pathogen depends on for sustenance.

Insecticidal soap. Specially formulated solutions of fatty acids that kill insect pests like aphids, mites, and whiteflies.

Instar. The form of an insect between each molt. Most insects pass through three to six instars.

Larva. An immature stage of an insect.

Maggot. The larva of a fly, usually a small, white, legless worm without an obvious head. Mouthparts are hooked.

Milky disease spores. A microbial insecticide that kills Japanese beetle grubs.

Molt. A shedding of the exoskeleton so that an insect can grow. The old skin splits after a new one has formed beneath it.

Nematode. A microscopic, unsegmented, threadlike worm; some nematodes are beneficial, while others can harm plants.

Nymph. An immature stage of an insect that doesn't form a pupa.

Organic matter. Materials that are derived directly from plants or animals. Organic gardeners use plant and animal by-products to maintain soil and plant health and don't rely on synthetically made fertilizers, herbicides, or pesticides.

Organic pest management. An approach to pest control that combines cultural, biological, and physical measures to prevent problems or to keep them in check.

Parasite. An insect that lives and feeds in or on another insect or animal for at least part of its life cycle.

Pathogen. An organism that causes disease.

Pesticide. Any substance, synthetic or natural, that is used to kill insects, animals, fungi, bacteria, or weeds.

Pheromone. A chemical substance, such as a sexual attractant, secreted by an insect to create a response in others of its species.

Pheromone traps. Insect traps that work by attracting male insects to the scent of breeding female insects. These traps are available for a variety of flying pests, including cabbage loopers, Japanese beetles, and peachtree borers. The traps work best in large areas or orchards.

Physical controls. Control measures that prevent pests from reaching your plants or remove them if they do. Barriers, traps, and hand-picking are physical controls.

Predator. An insect that feeds on another live insect or animal.

Pupa. A hardened shell formed by a larva, within which the adult stage develops.

Row covers. Sheets of lightweight, permeable material, usually polypropylene or polyester, that can be laid loosely on top of plants to act as a barrier to insect pests or that can give a few degrees of frost protection at the beginning or end of the growing season

Scavenger. An insect that feeds on dead plants, animals, or decaying matter.

Spiracle. One of many tiny holes in the thorax and abdomen of an insect that serve as breathing pores.

Summer oil. A light petroleum oil that controls aphids, mealybugs, spider mites, scales, and some caterpillars. For use on ornamentals. See also Dormant oil.

Thorax. The center section of an insect's body, between the head and the abdomen. Wings and legs are attached to the thorax.

Trap crops. Plants you grow to lure pests away from other crops in your beds. For example, dill lures tomato hornworms away from tomatoes.

Virus. Microscopic organisms that must be inside the living cell of a host to reproduce. Viruses can be transmitted by insects, mites, and nematodes as well as through contact with garden tools and plant cuttings.

Viviparous. Bearing live young. Aphids can be viviparous.

Recommended Reading & Resources

Books & Periodicals

Benjamin, Joan, and Deborah Martin, eds. *Great Garden Formulas.* Emmaus, PA: Rodale, 1998.

Bradley, Fern Marshall, and Barbara Ellis, eds. *Rodale's All-New Encyclopedia of Organic Gardening.* Emmaus, PA: Rodale, 1992

Bradley, Fern Marshall, ed. *Rodale's Chemical-Free Yard and Garden.* Emmaus, PA: Rodale, 1991.

Ellis, Barbara W., and Fern Marshall Bradley. *The Organic Gardener's Handbook of Natural Insect and Disease Control.* Emmaus, PA: Rodale, 1996.

Flint, M. L. *Pests of the Garden and Small Farm: A Grower's Guide to Using Less Pesticide.* Oakland, CA: University of California, 1998.

Gilkeson, Linda, et al. *Rodale's Pest and Disease Problem Solver.* Emmaus, PA: Rodale, 1996.

Hart, Rhonda. *Bugs, Slugs, and Other Thugs.* Pownal, VT: Storey Communications, 1991.

Olkowski, William, et al. *The Gardener's Guide to Common-Sense Pest Control.* Newtown, CT: The Taunton Press, 1995.

Organic Gardening, Rodale Inc., 33 E. Minor Street, Emmaus, PA 18098

Pleasant, Barbara. *The Gardener's Guide to Plant Diseases.* Pownal, VT: Storey Communications, 1995.

Pleasant, Barbara. *The Gardener's Bug Book.* Pownal, VT: Storey Communications, 1994.

Smith, Miranda, and Anna Carr. *Rodale's Garden Insect, Disease & Weed Identification Guide.* Emmaus, PA: Rodale, 1988.

Smittle, Delilah, ed. *Rodale's Complete Garden Problem Solver.* Emmaus, PA: Rodale, 1997.

Westcott, Cynthia. *The Gardener's Bug Book.* Garden City, NY: Doubleday & Company, 1973.

Tools & Supplies

Applied Bionomics Ltd.
11074 West Saanich Road
Sidney, BC, V8L 5P5
Canada
Phone: (604) 656-2123
Fax: (604) 656-3844

Arbico Environmentals
P.O. Box 4247 CRB
Tucson, AZ 85738
Phone: (520) 825-9785
Fax: (520) 825-2038
E-mail: info@arbico.com
Web site: www.arbico.com

Beneficial Insectary
9664 Tanqueray Court
Redding, CA 96003
Phone: (800) 477-3715
Fax: (888) 472-0708
E-mail: bi@insectary.com
Web site: www.insectary.net

Better Yield Insects
44 Bristol Road
Narragansett, RI 02882
Phone: (800) 662-6562
Fax: (401) 792-8085

Buena Biosystems
P.O. Box 4008
Ventura, CA 95340
Phone: (805) 525-2525
Fax: (805) 525-6058
E-mail: bugdude@msn.com

Foothill Agricultural Research
510 West Chase Drive
Corona, CA 91720
Phone: (909) 371-0120
Fax: (909) 279-5150

Gardener's Supply Co.
128 Intervale Road
Burlington, VT 05404
Phone: (800) 863-1700
Fax: (800) 551-6712
E-mail: Info@gardeners.com
Web site: www.gardeners.com

Gardens Alive!
5100 Schenley Place
Lawrenceburg, IN 47025
Phone: (812) 537-8650
Fax: (812) 537-5108
E-mail: gardenhelp@gardens-alive.com
Web site: www.gardens-alive.com

The Green Spot, Ltd.
93 Priest Road
Nottingham, NH 03290-6204
Phone: (603) 942-8925
Fax: (603) 942-8932
E-mail: info@greenmethods.com
Web site: www.greenmethods.com

Harmony Farm Supply
P.O. Box 460
Graton, CA 95444
Phone: (707) 823-9125
Fax: (707) 823-1734
E-mail: info@harmonyfarm.com
Web site: www.harmonyfarm.com

Hydro-Gardens
P.O. Box 25845
Colorado Springs, CO 80936
Phone: (800) 634-6362
Fax: (719) 495-2266
E-mail: hgi@usa.net
Web site: www.hydro-gardens.com

Johnny's Selected Seeds
Foss Hill Road
Albion, ME 04910
Phone: (207) 437-4301
Fax: (207) 437-2165; (800) 437-4290
E-mail: johnnys@johnnyseeds.com
Web site: www.johnnyseeds.com

The LadyBug Company
8706 Oro-Quincy Highway
Berry Creek, CA 95916
Phone: (916) 589-5227

The Natural Gardening Company
P.O. Box 750776
Petaluma, CA 94975
Phone: (707) 766-9303
Fax: (707) 766-9747
E-mail: info@naturalgardening.com
Web site: www.naturalgardening.com

Natural Insect Control
RR#2
Stevensville, Ontario, Canada L0S 1S0
Phone: (905) 382-2904
Fax: (905) 382-4418
E-mail: nic@niagara.com
Web site: www.natural-insect-control.com

Nature's Control
P.O. Box 35
Medford, OR 97501
Phone: (541) 245-6033
Fax: (800) 698-6250
E-mail: info@naturescontrol.com
Web site: www.naturescontrol.com

Peaceful Valley Farm Supply
P.O. Box 2209
Grass Valley, CA 95945
Phone: (888) 784-1722; (530) 272-4769
Fax: (530) 272-4794
E-mail: contact@groworganic.com
Web site: www.groworganic.com

Planet Natural
1612 Gold Avenue
Bozeman, MT 59715
Phone: (800) 289-6656; (406) 587-5891
Fax: (406) 587-0223
E-mail: ecostore@mcn.net
Web site: www.planetnatural.com

Rincon-Vitova Insectaries
P.O. Box 1555
Ventura, CA 93002
Phone: (800) 248-2847
Fax: (805) 643-6267
E-mail: bugnet@rinconvitova.com
Web site: www.rinconvitova.com

Smith & Hawken
Two Arbor Lane
Box 6900
Florence, KY 41022
Phone: (800) 940-1170
E-mail: smithandhawkencustomer
    service@discovery.com
Web site: www.smith-hawken.com

Territorial Seed Co.
P.O. Box 157
Cottage Grove, OR 97424
Phone: (541) 942-9547
Fax: (888) 657-3131
E-mail: tertrl@srv1.vsite.com
Web site: www.territorial-seed.com

Worm's Way
7850 North Highway 37
Bloomington, IN 47404
Phone: (800) 598-8158
Fax: (800) 316-1306
E-mail: catalog@wormsway.com
Web site: www.wormsway.com

Acknowledgments

Contributors to this book include Lynn Byczynski, Jill Jesiolowski Cebenko, Cheryl Long, Barbara Pleasant, Joanna Poncavage, Porter Shimer, and Catherine Yronwode.

Photo Credits

AG Stock 48, 58, 62

Matthew Benson 2 (*top*)

Rob Cardillo iv, 30, 93 (*top*)

David Cavagnaro 12 (*bottom*), 28 (*bottom*), 74

Walter Chandoha vi, 4, 60, 78

Corbis 85

Alan and Linda Detrick 34, 56, 80, 93 (*bottom*)

James Dill 38

John Glover 86

Russell R. Grundke 83

Bill Johnson 32, 40, 70

Kit Latham 17

David Liebman 90

Mitch Mandel 2 (*bottom*), 14, 21, 23, 24, 27

Positive Images/Patricia J. Bruno 54, 92

Positive Images/Karen Bussolini 22, 66

Positive Images/Albert Squillace 12 (*top left*)

Rodale Stock Images 7

Richard Shiell 72, 88

Rob and Ann Simpson 82

Steven Foster Group/Martin Wall 5 (*bottom*)

Mark Turner 11, 12 (*top right*), 12 (*middle*), 18

Chuck Weight i, 5 (*top*), 13, 26, 28 (*top*), 42, 52, 81, 84, 89

Ron West 36, 44, 46, 68, 76

Rick Wetherbee 3, 6, 8, 25, 50, 64, 91, 94–95

Index

M

Mating disruption, 24
Mealybugs, 27
Mexican bean beetles, 13, 60–61, *60*
Mice, 82, *82*
Milkweed, 53
Mint, 12, 13
Mites
    beneficial, 69
    controlling, 24, 26, 27
Moles, 82
Monarch butterfly, 5
Mulch, 17
Mustard, 12, 28, 53

N

Nematodes, 29
Nicotine, 25

O

Oriental fruit moths, 63
Overwintering
    diseases, 92
    pests, 3, 16–17 (*See also
        specific pests*)

P

Parasitic wasps, 12, 49
Peachtree borers, 62–63, *62*
Peppers, 89, 91
Perennials, 5, *5*, 49, 88
Pesticides
    botanical, 25
    chemical, 1–2, 13
    water as, 27, 75
Petunias, *11*
Pheromone traps, 23–24, *23*
Planning, 4, 31
Plants
    crowding, 5, 15
    mixing in garden, 4, *4*
    pest repellent, 4
    pest resistant, 5, *5*, 15
    as traps, 28–29, *28*, 41
Potatoes, 57, 92
Pot marigold, 13

Purple coneflower *(Echinacea
    purpurea)*, 5, *5*
Pyrethrum, 25

R

Rabbits, 81, *81*
Raccoons, 84, *84*
Radishes, 28
Raised beds, 10, 90
Record keeping, 16
Red fescue, 51
Repellent plants, 4
Repellents. *See specific animal pests*
Resistant plants, 5, *5*, 15
Rhododendrons, 87
Rootworms, corn, 7
Roses, 55, 75, 87
Rotenone, 25
Rove beetles, 39
Ryania, 25

S

Sabadilla, 25
Salt injury, 88
Salvia, *11*
Scales
    controlling, 22, 26–27
    profile, 64–65, *64*
Scarecrows, 85, *85*
Seasonal pest-fighting calendar, 94–95
Site selection, 9–11, *11*
Slugs
    "bug" type, 29
    controlling, 13, 67
    profile, 66–67, *66*
    toads and, 47
Snails, 29, 66–67, *66*
Soft scales, 64–65, *64. See also* Scales
Soil
    compacted, 11
    waterlogged, 90, *90*
Soil amendments, *2*
Soil testing, 15
Spider mites
    controlling, 27, 75
    profile, 68–69, *68*
Spined soldier bugs, 53

USDA Plant Hardiness Zone Map

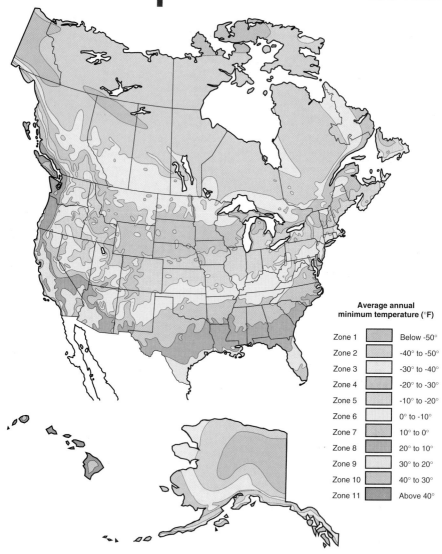

Average annual minimum temperature (°F)

Zone		Temperature
Zone 1		Below -50°
Zone 2		-40° to -50°
Zone 3		-30° to -40°
Zone 4		-20° to -30°
Zone 5		-10° to -20°
Zone 6		0° to -10°
Zone 7		10° to 0°
Zone 8		20° to 10°
Zone 9		30° to 20°
Zone 10		40° to 30°
Zone 11		Above 40°

This map was revised in 1990 and is recognized as the best indicator of minimum temperatures available. Look at the map to find your area, then match its color to the key. When you've found your color, the key will tell you what hardiness zone you live in. Remember that the map is a general guide; your particular conditions may vary.